MURDER MOST CRYPTIC

The PUZZLING
Casebook of a Curious
Country Village

igl00books

Written by Rose Harkness, Helen Catt and Emily Bruce
Illustrated by Giuliano Aloisi

Designed by Richard Sykes
Edited by Katie Taylor

Copyright © 2021 Igloo Books Ltd

Published in 2022
First published in the UK by Igloo Books Ltd
An imprint of Igloo Books Ltd
Cottage Farm, NN6 0BJ, UK
Owned by Bonnier Books
Sveavägen 56, Stockholm, Sweden

Manufactured in China. 0322 001
10 9 8 7 6 5 4 3 2 1

Library of Congress Cataloging-in-Publication
Data is available upon request.

ISBN 978-1-80108-654-7
IglooBooks.com
bonnierbooks.co.uk

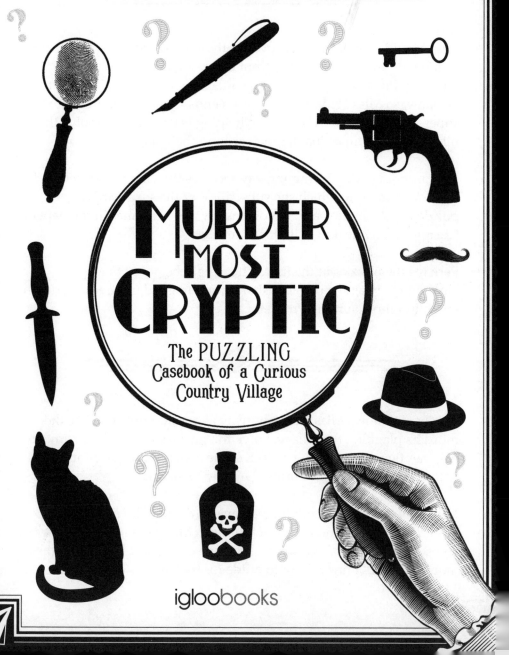

MURDER MOST CRYPTIC

The PUZZLING
Casebook of a Curious
Country Village

igloobooks

ABOUT THIS BOOK

Miss Matilda Hemmingway loves nothing more than to spend a quiet evening doing brainteasers in front of her log fire in the cozy country village of Puzzleby. Unfortunately, Puzzleby does rather live up to its name, so Miss Hemmingway often ends up having to put her super-sleuthing skills to good use helping D.C. Copper to solve the misdemeanor crimes that happen around the village.

Each morning, Miss Hemmingway receives the village newsletter, *The Puzzleby Gazette*, to which she subscribes for the surprisingly good puzzle section in the back. Unfortunately, the headlines in the paper of late are usually dealing with local murders.

Perhaps the puzzles in the newsletter might be of use to Miss Hemmingway as she puts her sharp mind to good use tracking down the murderers haunting Puzzleby...

This book follows Miss Hemmingway as she attempts to solve the murders plaguing the village. Solve the puzzles within each crime to help her figure out the clues. Each crime comes with space for you to note your suspicions and bring the killer to justice.

You'll see that Miss Hemmingway enjoys the puzzles in *The Puzzleby Gazette*. Someone has left hints in Miss Hemmingway's copy, and solving these will give her a message that will help her find the murderer. You'll find a how-to guide for the puzzles on page 6.

CONTENTS

PUZZLE INSTRUCTIONS

A TO Z PUZZLE
Each letter of the alphabet from A to Z has been removed from the grid once, to leave 26 empty squares. You must work out which letter from A to Z fits in each of the blank squares, and write it in so as to fill the grid and solve the puzzle.

ARROW WORDS
Answer the clues in the grid in the direction of each arrow to complete the puzzle.

BATTLESHIPS
Locate the position of each of the ships listed in the grid. Numbers around the edge tell you the number of ship segments in each row and column of the puzzle. Ships are surrounded on all sides by water, including diagonally.

BRIDGES
Connect all the circles (which represent islands) into a single interconnected group. The number in a circle represents the number of bridges that connect that island to other islands. Bridges can only be created horizontally or vertically, with no more than two bridges between any pair of islands. Bridges cannot cross any other bridges.

JIGSAW SUDOKU
Place the numbers 1–9 once in each row, column and bold-lined jigsaw region composed of nine units.

KAKURO
Fill the white squares so that the total in each across or down run of units matches the total at the start of that run. You must use the numbers from 1–9 only and cannot repeat a number in a run.

KING'S JOURNEY

Figure out the journey of a chess king as it visits each square of the grid exactly once, starting at 1 and ending at 100. The king may move one square in any direction at a time, including diagonally.

KRISS KROSS

Each word must be placed in the grid once to solve the puzzle – you must work out where each word goes in order to complete the grid.

PATHFINDER

Moving from letter to adjacent letter, find a path that visits every square and spells out words associated with the given theme. Start on the shaded square.

RECTANGLES

Divide the grid into a series of rectangles or squares, such that every cell is in exactly one region. Numbers indicate the size of each region: for instance a '5' in a cell means that cell is part of a region that contains five cells in total. There is only one number in each region.

SUDOKU

Place the numbers 1–9 once in each row, column and nine-unit square.

A NOTE:

Miss Hemmingway will also have riddles and codes to solve. Any number puzzles in the newsletter sections give letters in a standard A1 Z26 code:

A = 1
B = 2
Z = 26

PUZZLEBY VILLAGE

DALLIANCE RESIDENCE

MISS HEMMINGWAY'S HOUSE

THE CHAPEL

VILLAGE HALL

LIBRARY

LAKE CALAMITY

THE MURDERED PINT

CHARACTERS

MISS HEMMINGWAY

Miss Hemmingway might seem easily overlooked, but her mind is as sharp as a tack. An established spinster, she lives in the cozy village of Puzzleby with her companions, Baskerville and Cat. She has a penchant for puzzles, and doing the daily brain teaser in the newsletter is the highlight of her day.

BASKERVILLE

Baskerville is her beloved basset hound, and he's always up for some juicy meat from the butchers. Though getting on in years, he's very good at following trails—as long as you point him in the right direction...

CAT

Cat is Miss Hemmingway's feline friend. He's a bit persnickety, and can often be found patrolling his territory along Miss Hemmingway's garden fence or preening his silky paws. He's not too keen on the neighbors after Dahliah Dalliance refused him a piece of sardine.

CHARACTERS

DAHLIAH DALLIANCE

Dahliah is Miss Hemmingway's neighbor and a rising mystery novelist, famed for adding a sexy, supernatural twist to her books. She's the village gossip, and can often be found sticking her nose into everybody's business.

DEIRDRE DALLIANCE

Deirdre is Dahliah's teenage daughter, and publishes the village newsletter, *The Puzzleby Gazette*, with her friends. She's a bit awkward and can be moody at times, but she's a lovely girl and Miss Hemmingway likes her. So does Cat (though not if her mother's around!).

D. C. COPPER

D. C. Copper is the local policeman. He doesn't have a lot to do in such a sleepy village, so his days often pass in a blur of morning tea breaks and afternoon naps. He has a soft spot for Miss Hemmingway, whom he often consults on such crimes as: "Who stole my last biscuit?" (It was Baskerville…)

CHARACTERS

JOHN THE BEEKEEPER

John is well known for being the best beekeeper in Puzzleby. He supplies the local grocers with honey, which often sells out. His schoolteacher niece, Liza, also lives in the village and shares his love of beekeeping herself.

JACQUES BROCHET

Jacques Brochet is the five-times champion of Le Tournoi de Pêche Paris, and the three-times champion of the Tournoi de Pêche au Lac de la Tête d'Or in Lyon. He claims there is no fish too slippery for his line, and he intends to prove it in the Lake Calamity Fish-Off at Puzzleby.

PAULA ELSTREE

Paula Elstree is the local celebrity baker, often employed to judge the competitions held in the village. A high-five from Paula is much coveted! Her specialities are a divine Black Forest Gâteau that causes long lines at the summer gala, and an olive ciabatta that won the prestigious Taste of Italy rosette.

CHARACTERS

SAM HAGGLE

Sam Haggle is Puzzleby's town planner. He's in charge of making sure the village is a great place to visit and approving plans for new buildings, statues, paths etc. Unfortunately, he's a big believer in newer being better, which can ruffle a few feathers in the sleepy little village…

FATHER FEATHERBY

103-year-old Father Featherby is Puzzleby's respected priest and heads up the church. His Yuletide services draw people in from across the village, and you can always go to him for some good advice, whether that be on relationship issues, cabbage growing, or knitting patterns.

CASE ONE:

THE

BEEKEEPER'S

HIVES

INTRODUCTION

IT WAS A SLOW SUNNY DAY IN PUZZLEBY. I was sitting out in my garden enjoying the buzzing of the late summer bees around the lavender. Dear Dahliah Dalliance, my neighbor, swatted at the glistening jug of iced lemonade.

"How am I supposed to work with all these awful bees following me around the place?" she sighed. She gave one last swat, and her glass spilled all across her notebook. "Darn. So much for Chapter Three: The Hero's Bicep." Before I could commiserate, young Deirdre came down the road on her paper route. "It's so good to see young people really applying themselves, don't you think?" Dahliah said with a sniff. "Although I do wish you wouldn't scowl quite so much, dear," she added as Deirdre approached my gate.

Deirdre handed me *The Puzzleby Gazette* over the gate, ignoring her mother. I sat by the lavender and immediately opened up the newsletter to the puzzle section.

Just then, I saw D.C. Copper, his police helmet at an angle that can only be described as "disheartened". He saw me and made a beeline to the gate.

"Something the matter, D.C. Copper?" I asked.

"Have you heard the news of John the Beekeeper's death?" he asked.

"A tragic incident, I heard," chimed in Dahliah. "So ironic. A beekeeper, stung to death by his own bees."

"That's what the coroner believes," D.C. Copper said. "But something about it doesn't quite sit right with me. John's the best beekeeper in Puzzleby! All the honey at Bessie Pygott's store comes from his hives. Why would they suddenly attack?"

"You surely don't suspect..." Dahliah threw a glance side-to-side before whispering loudly, "...MURDER?"

"Whatever I suspect, it doesn't matter. The case will be closed if I can't find any evidence before the end of the day." He gave a forlorn sigh. "Well, I suppose I'll keep looking."

It wasn't until he had walked away that I noticed the piece of paper that had fallen from the file he was carrying. I picked it up and folded it neatly. I would bring it by the police station when I took Baskerville on his walk.

THE BEEKEEPER'S HIVES

OF COURSE, DEAR JOHN'S UNTIMELY DEATH was very tragic, but the circumstances were really none of my business. I sat down to do a puzzle, while Cat engaged in some lightharded murder of his own, in the form of a small woolly mouse that needed disembowelling. However, as I baffled, something strange about the letters in the gray squares caught my attention. I began to wonder if there might be a message there.

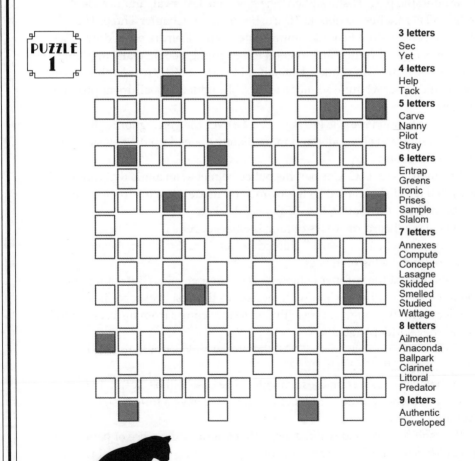

PUZZLE 1

3 letters
Sec
Yet

4 letters
Help
Tack

5 letters
Carve
Nanny
Pilot
Stray

6 letters
Entrap
Greens
Ironic
Prises
Sample
Slalom

7 letters
Annexes
Compute
Concept
Lasagne
Skidded
Smelled
Studied
Wattage

8 letters
Ailments
Anaconda
Ballpark
Clarinet
Littoral
Predator

9 letters
Authentic
Developed

THE BEEKEEPER'S HIVES

I NOTED ALL THE LETTERS FROM THE PUZZLE carefully in the pattern. Alas, it was a mere jumble of letters. But perhaps there was something to be unraveled...

PUZZLE 2

___ ___ ___   ___ ___   ___ ___ ___ ___

___ ___ ___ ___ ___ ___

___ ___ ___   ___ ___   ___ ___ ___ ___

___ ___ ___ ___ ___ ___

Well, that was enough to get me off my chair!

"Come now, Baskerville," I said. He gave a wide yawn, and obediently waddled to heel. Off we went to look into this business a little more closely.

THE BEEKEEPER'S HIVES

PEOPLE PAY LITTLE ATTENTION to a lady such as myself walking an elderly basset hound, so I reached the alleged scene of the crime unchecked. The Beekeeper's gate was held fast by a rather large padlock, of remarkable weight and unusual design.

The mechanism was a three digit code. For a while I was stumped. While I pondered, I took out the puzzle page of the village newspaper to spark the little gray cells. I soon noticed something unusual about that week's sudoku. Perhaps, I thought to myself, this puzzle was the key...

PUZZLE 3

	1	5		3	6			
		9	1	4			3	
6	▓	3					▓	1
			5				8	
	5	6	8	▓	4	3	1	
	2				3			
7						8		6
	6			7	1	9		
			6	5		1	7	

THE BEEKEEPER'S HIVES

THE GATE CREAKED OPEN, so to avoid prying eyes, I slipped inside quickly. It is such a displeasure to have nosy neighbors, don't you think? Baskerville at once began to pull me around the garden with quite uncharacteristic vigor.

Of course, being the elderly hound that he is, he can only move quite slowly and is rather prone to becoming distracted, so it took us a while before we found the source of his sniffs.

	51								66
49	52	54		61	87		70		
						90			
	30		59	98					
				100	97			83	
15		26		45	94	93	82		74
								78	
	8			24	34		77		40
	5			20					
1				11			36		

PUZZLE 4

Figure out the journey of the elderly hound as he visits each square of the grid exactly once, starting at 1 and ending at 100. Baskerville may move one square in any direction at a time, including diagonally.

THE BEEKEEPER'S HIVES

THE ENTRANCE TO JOHN'S ORCHARD was quite overgrown, and I would not have spotted it if it weren't for Baskerville's tugging. There were some obvious changes from the last time I had visited the orchard, just a week before — the body-shaped hollow in the grass, for one. But I thought perhaps there were some other changes, too.

THE BEEKEEPER'S HIVES

Can you find the eight differences between the two scenes?

THE BEEKEEPER'S HIVES

WE **CONTINUED** past the gate of Frederick Bailey, cobbler and aspiring apiarist, from where came a snuffling noise, not unlike Baskerville after he has had a bath forced upon him.

"Perhaps the hive had lost their queen," Frederick snuffled between sobs. "That can make them angry." He thrust a somewhat damp scrap of paper at me, before going back to pruning his roses. It was time for my morning tea, so I sat on the bench by the village green with my flask and distracted myself with an entertaining puzzle from the newsletter.

PUZZLE 6

Arrow words puzzle clues (as they appear in the grid):

- Seventh Greek letter
- Poker stake
- Repeated jazz phrase
- Jewelled headdress
- House with one storey
- Neutral
- Not inclined to talk
- Fish appendage
- Topic
- Male person
- Mineral spring
- Character in Oliver Twist
- Rough or harsh sound
- Sues (anag)
- Bright patch of colour
- Strong lightweight wood
- Saline
- Belonging to us
- Vertical spar on a ship
- Olajuwon: Basketball player
- Minnelli: US actress
- Damp
- Alleviate
- Item used in cricket
- ___ Thurman: actress
- Scoop water out of a boat
- Form of public transport
- Shola ___: singer
- Franz ___: Hungarian composer
- Animal fodder
- Light brown colour

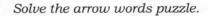

Solve the arrow words puzzle.

THE BEEKEEPER'S HIVES

BRAIN SUITABLY RECHARGED, I turned my attention to the list of names and numbers that Frederick Bailey had given me. It was a scrappy piece of paper, and seemed to be written on the back of someone's chemistry homework. Unfortunately, in Frederick's distress, several of the names and numbers were smudged out by his tears. However, I spied a doodle in the corner of the paper that I could use to help me figure out which number to call first...

PUZZLE
7

Can you work out which person Miss Hemmingway needs to ring?

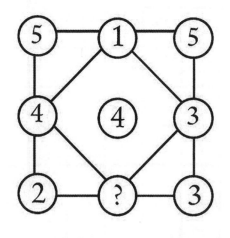

1. Rory Newton - 515-443-223
2. Billy Mead - 515-443-253
3. Heather Barber - 515-443-266
4. Liza Liszt - 515-443-263
5. Raj Copper - 515-443-254
6. Eileen Blake - 515-443-113

PUZZLEBY GAZETTE
VILLAGE NEWSLETTER

PUZZLE
8

Solve all the puzzles from the Puzzleby Gazette to reveal a message about the crime in question.

						8		
	1		3				4	
3		5	2		4			7
	9							
		8				7		
	3	7	8					
		3						
				2		6		

Revenge of the Busty Beekeeper by Dahliah Dalliance

The first romantic thriller from Puzzleby's bestselling crime author. Ffion Honey just wants to make blackberry honey, as her family has done for generations. New farmer Andy Widnes has other ideas. But when Andy's brother Nick is found drowned in a honey barrel, Ffion finds herself thrown into a murder investigation…

PUZZLEBY GAZETTE
VILLAGE NEWSLETTER

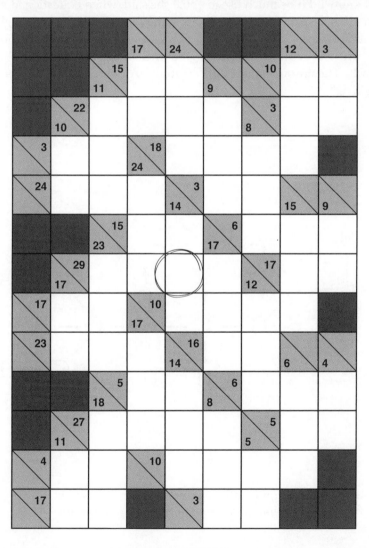

I FELT THAT THE PUZZLE was advising me to visit Liza Liszt, a young schoolteacher who smelled faintly of lemon drops. She was in her garden, inspecting a set of newly painted hives.

I don't know if I'll be much use to you," she said, when I questioned her about John's death. "I'm very new to beekeeping, I'm afraid." I caught sight of a large, imposing textbook. "I'm a biology teacher," she explained. "Did you know, when a bee stings something, the smell of the sting attracts other bees to attack? They're such interesting creatures. Ah—sorry, perhaps that was insensitive."

PUZZLE
10

Which of the symbols on the paper from Frederick matches the chemical symbol of the bee pheromone?

THE BEEKEEPER'S HIVES

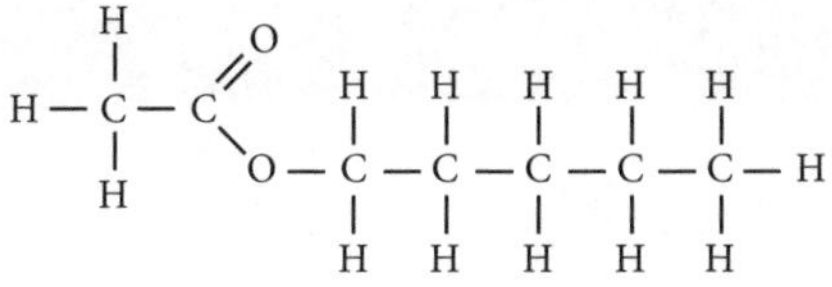

pentyl acetate (pears)

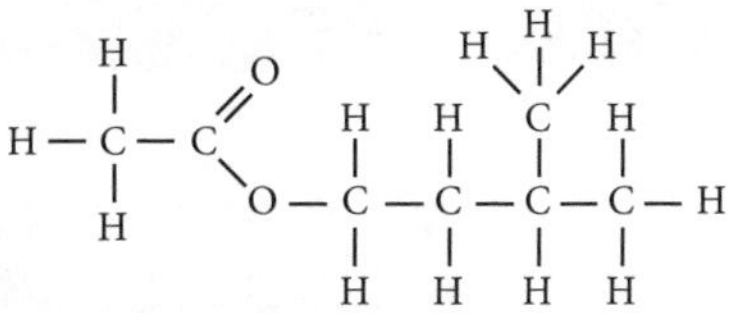

3-methylbutyl acetate (bananas)

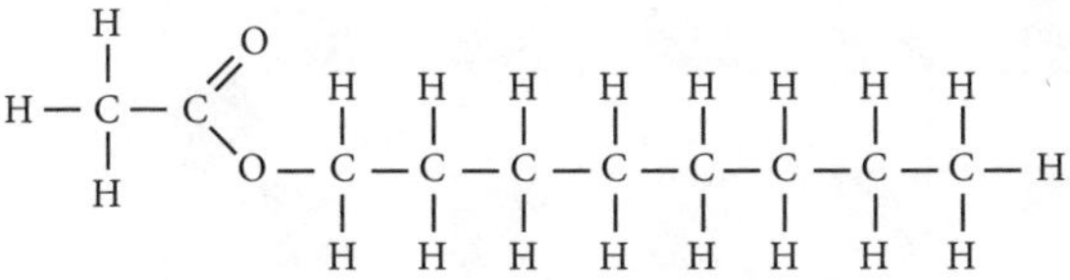

octyl acetate (oranges)

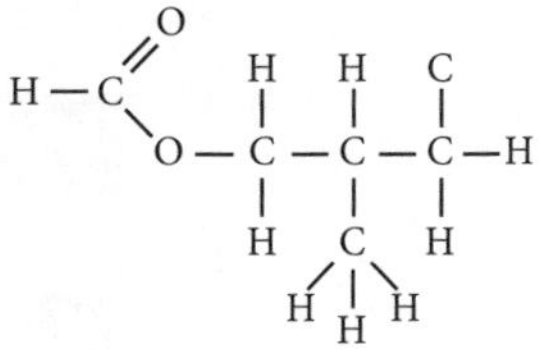

methylpropyl formate (raspberry)

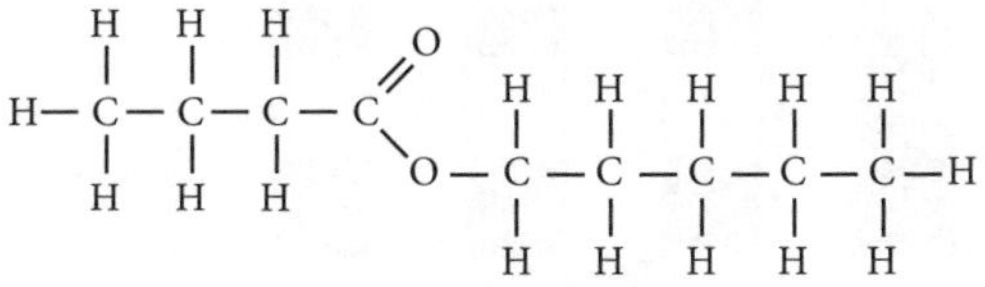

pentyl butyrate (apricot, strawberry)

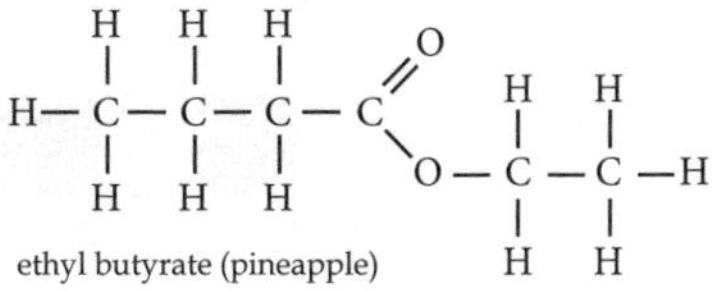

ethyl butyrate (pineapple)

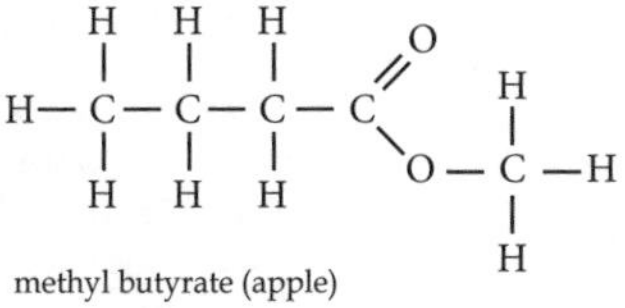

methyl butyrate (apple)

PUZZLE SECTION

PUZZLE 2

Across

1 Having inherent ability (4)
3 Plasters (anag) (8)
9 Go forward (7)
10 Crisp; pleasantly cold (5)
11 Poorly fed (12)
13 Deny of food (6)
15 ___ Cuthbert: actress (6)
17 Lacking courage (5-7)
20 At that place; not here (5)
21 Combining (7)
22 Waver (8)
23 Go by an indirect route (4)

Down

1 Creating needless panic (8)
2 Floor of a building (5)
4 Speculative view (6)
5 US state (12)
6 Convey a thought in words (7)
7 Utters (4)
8 Awkward (12)
12 Secured with a dressing (8)
14 Wolfgang ___ Mozart: composer (7)
16 Push forcefully (6)
18 In a ___ : very quickly (5)
19 Engrave; carve (4)

PUZZLE SECTION

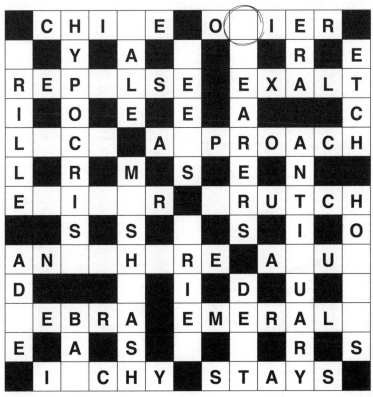

PUZZLE
3

A B C D E F G H I J K L M N O P Q R S T U V W X Y Z

THE BEEKEEPER'S HIVES

SOMEWHAT SUSPICIOUS, I continued to question Miss Liszt. "Where did you get your queen, if you don't mind me asking?" If she was aware of my suspicions, Miss Liszt did not give any sign. She answered quite cheerfully. "From the Apiary Society. They're a little secretive, and not very trusting of strangers, but luckily dear old Uncle John put in a good word."

"Would you mind if I spoke to them directly?" I asked.

"Of course—the number is by the phone, but I'm afraid it's in code."

PUZZLE
13

```
        B   E   E
  +
        B   E   E
  _____

    S   E   N   D
```

—— —— —— —— —— —— ——

If "S" = 1 and "B" = 8, , reveal the phone number for the Apiary Society.

THE BEEKEEPER'S HIVES

THE APIARY SOCIETY, once I got through to them, confirmed Miss Liszt's story. To be sure, I felt I should do what I had previously avoided, and take a closer look at the beekeeper's hives. Baskerville and I returned to John's orchard, and, sucking the lemon drop that Miss Liszt had offered me for courage, I lifted the top of the hive and peered inside to look for the unique queen.

PUZZLE
14

Find the queen among the workers and the drones.

PUZZLEBY GAZETTE
VILLAGE NEWSLETTER

PUZZLE
15

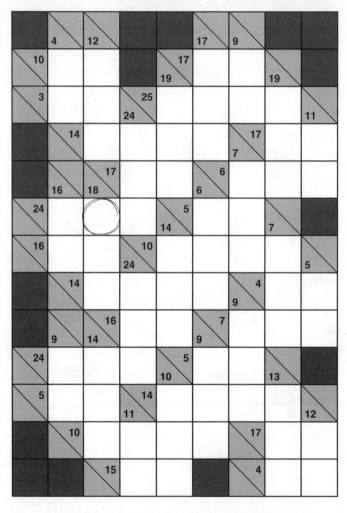

PUZZLEBY GAZETTE

VILLAGE NEWSLETTER

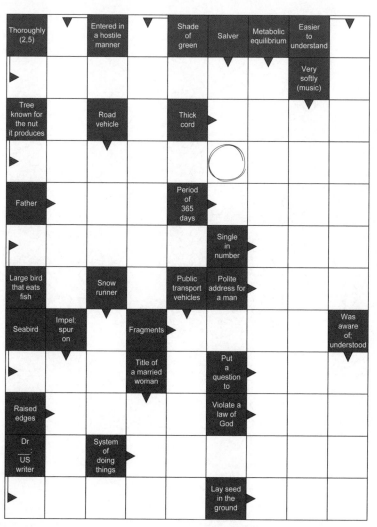

The crossword grid contains the following clues:

Clue	
Thoroughly (2,5)	
Entered in a hostile manner	
Shade of green	
Salver	
Metabolic equilibrium	
Easier to understand	
Very softly (music)	
Tree known for the nut it produces	
Road vehicle	
Thick cord	
Father	
Period of 365 days	
Single in number	
Large bird that eats fish	
Snow runner	
Public transport vehicles	
Polite address for a man	
Seabird	
Impel; spur on	
Fragments	
Was aware of; understood	
Title of a married woman	
Put a question to	
Raised edges	
Violate a law of God	
Dr ___: US writer	
System of doing things	
Lay seed in the ground	

33

THE BEEKEEPER'S HIVES

I WAS RATHER STUMPED. It was beginning to look like poor
John's death was a freak accident afterall. Miss Liszt had mentioned that
sometimes, if the queen is trapped, she can release pheromones that drive the
rest of the bees to attack. A little nervously, I looked closer at the hive and its
organisation.

PUZZLE
17

THE BEEKEEPER'S HIVES

Is the queen able to leave her hive?
Solve the maze to find out if she is trapped.

PUZZLEBY GAZETTE
VILLAGE NEWSLETTER

PUZZLE 18

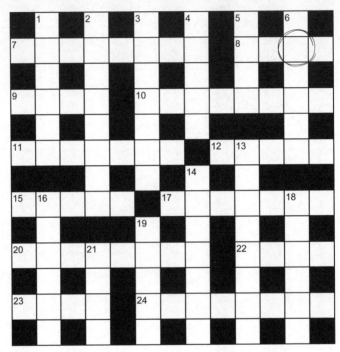

Across

7 Item used to remember the page you're on (8)
8 Cereal grains (4)
9 Bend or coil (4)
10 Waste disposal site (8)
11 In the place of (7)
12 English cricket ground (5)
15 Amusing (5)
17 Zephyrs (7)
20 Farewell appearance (8)
22 Ten-cent coin (US) (4)
23 Bivalve sea creature (4)
24 Orderliness (8)

Down

1 Vertical pillar (6)
2 The bones of the body (8)
3 Warhead carried by a missile (7)
4 Odor releasing animal (5)
5 Foot of a horse (4)
6 Fashioned (6)
13 Exaggerated (8)
14 Calamity (7)
16 Ill (6)
18 Entangle (6)
19 Estimates the price of (5)
21 Deprived of sensation (4)

PUZZLE SECTION

PUZZLE 19

	3			9		2		
	5						1	9
	6	1	8					
7	4			3				
8								3
		6				7	8	
◯			9	8	3			
1	9					2		
	4		5			9		

REVEAL YOUR FUTURE AND KNOW YOUR FORTUNE IN A CRYSTAL-GAZING SESSION WITH ACHILLIA HEADLAND. Will your love life be abuzz with suitors? Is your beloved uncle faring well on the other side? Achillia Headland can divulge this information during a discreet appointment. Enquire at 133 Wisteria Avenue.

THE BEEKEEPER'S HIVES

I COULDN'T SPEND ALL DAY inspecting bees. Dismayed, I made my way to the grocery store to pick up some sardines for my beloved Cat. I inspected the jars of Rose Cottage Honey and Little Orchard Honey while I waited at the counter, and my eye fell on a couple of the grocer's order sheets. I am not usually engaged in acts of petty theft, but sometimes it's a necessity. While Bessie's back was turned, I quickly snatched both sheets. When I exited, fish in hand, I looked a little more closely at the lists. The first was the order sheet for Miss Liszt, while the second was that of Frederick Bailey.

Unscramble the words to discover Liza Liszt's grocery list.

PUZZLE 20

PMOES ODLRN

EWRJYBSYRL LRATE

ILAVCM EAR LICENA

DFO CTAO

SSIHRA TAYNPD

AGEIRBGRNED

AIAC NP OAUTOHCL

ETTUE PAUNBR

THE BEEKEEPER'S HIVES

Delete one letter from each pair to unravel the grocer's code for Frederick's list. For example, the code DB AO GL could be unraveled as D̶L U̶O G̶W to make DOG.

CL AH BE RE CR IQ UE ES

DP OL AT AS MT TO OE LS

EC GI SG HS

SA LA RI WD IK IN SE YS

BR RA IN AL EN PA SF

SL AC UO NL PE LS

WA IP PI JL DE FS

WF AE MN CS LD EF UY DK AC EL LE

YOUR HOROSCOPE
FROM ACHILLIA
HEADLAND

Life has been sweet lately, hasn't it? However, beware Mars coming into retrograde, as this can bring repressed rage to the surface, which could mean explosive events in your life. Your surroundings will be a hive of activity, but it's important not to concern yourself with such things. Focus on yourself. Eat some fresh fruit, indulge in nature's beauty, and take a moment to really become at peace with yourself.

	1							
			3					
8			4	5		1		
		9	5			6	7	8
1								2
3			7			5		
		2					9	
		7						

PUZZLEBY GAZETTE
VILLAGE NEWSLETTER

PUZZLE
23

Stage play	Tearing	Keep away from	——— Simpson: cartoon character	Small social insect	The day after today	▼		Untimely	▼
▶	▼	▼	▼	▼	Possess	▶			
___ Lendl: former tennis star	▶				Pull			Foreign language (informal)	
Small window on a ship	▶				▼				
Hog	▶			Song for a solo voice	▶				
▶									
Patches of facial hair		Particle that holds quarks together	Charming and elegant	Company symbol	▶				
▶		▼	▼	Was aware of; understood	Came first	▶			
Hens lay these	Third Gospel	▶		▼			Fall behind	Beer	
Chinese monetary unit	▶				Scientific workplace (abbrev)	▶	▼		
Rejuvenate	Generally; in summary	▶							
▶					Command to a horse	▶			

THE BEEKEEPER'S HIVES

NOW I FELT THAT I was getting somewhere. On my list of chores for the day, I also had to pop by the doctors' to renew my prescription, so Baskerville and I made our way to the surgery.

Peter, the receptionist, takes patient confidentiality very seriously, but he was kind enough to give me a couple of clues as to which file belonged to the poor late John.

PUZZLE 24

1. The second digit is more than double the first digit.

2. The number is not prime.

3. The number is not divisible by 2, 5 or 7.

4. The sum of the digits is 10 or greater.

51	52	53	54	55	56	57	58	59
41	42	43	44	45	46	47	48	49
31	32	33	34	35	36	37	38	39
21	22	23	24	25	26	27	28	29
11	12	13	14	15	16	17	18	19

Use Peter's clues to work out which file belongs to John the Beekeeper.

IOPENED UP THE **FILE,** and therein discovered the images taken from John's allergy tests. I matched them with the image I had borrowed from the police file earlier.

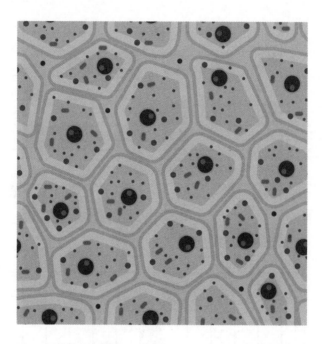

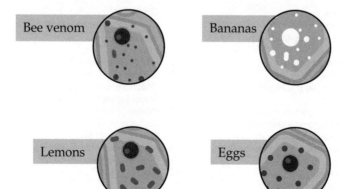

Bee venom

Bananas

Lemons

Eggs

PUZZLE
26

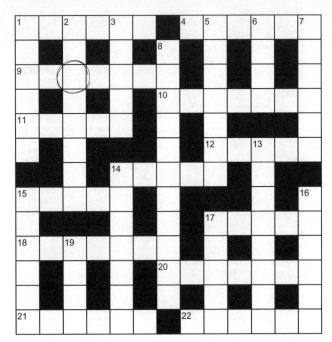

Across

1 Folk instrument (6)
4 Having only magnitude (of a quantity) (6)
9 The small details of something (7)
10 Large fortified buildings (7)
11 Frostily (5)
12 Famous English racetrack (5)
14 Electronic communication (5)
15 Fertile spots in deserts (5)
17 Crucial person or point; axis (5)
18 Capital of Kenya (7)
20 Subtleties (7)
21 Bright patch of color (6)
22 Stops (6)

Down

1 Country in central Africa (6)
2 Ringing in the ears (8)
3 Way in (5)
5 Close to the shore (7)
6 Quieten down; send to sleep (4)
7 Reddish-brown colour (6)
8 Travelling with a rucksack (11)
13 Narrow fissures (8)
14 Bodyguards (7)
15 Snow leopards (6)
16 Stagnation or inactivity (6)
17 Freedom from war (5)
19 Hero (4)

PUZZLEBY GAZETTE

VILLAGE NEWSLETTER

PUZZLE
27

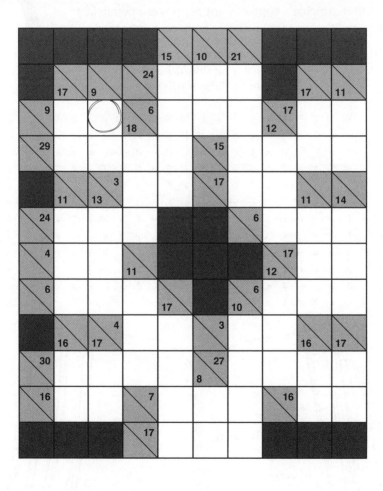

THE BEEKEEPER'S HIVES

HAVING FIGURED OUT what John was allergic to, I decided to look a little more closely at who might have stumbled across this crucial information. There was a date on the test results, from just a few weeks ago, and as luck would have it, Doctor Adichie's appointment diary was open to just the right page. It would take some decyphering, however.

PUZZLE 28

Decode the doctor's handwriting to discover who might have known about John's allergy.

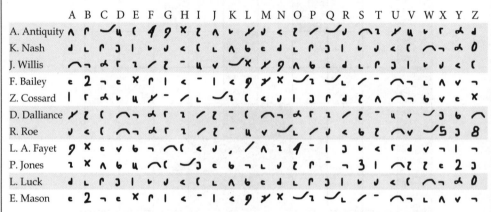

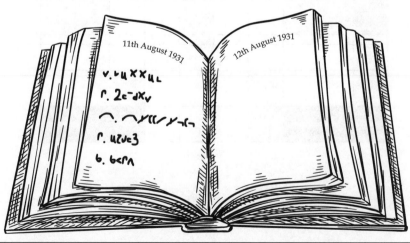

11th August 1931

12th August 1931

THE BEEKEEPER'S HIVES

THERE WAS ONE LAST piece of the puzzle I wanted to confirm before taking my conclusion to D.C. Copper. Searching through the newsletter again, I thought perhaps one of the puzzles may give me the clue I needed.

Ash, Aspen, Beech, Downy Birch, English Oak,
Field Maple, Grey Willow, Scots Pine, Sycamore,
Turkey Oak, White Poplar, Wild Cherry, Yew

Which tree on the list is not part of the answer to the puzzle?

PUZZLE SECTION

PUZZLE 30

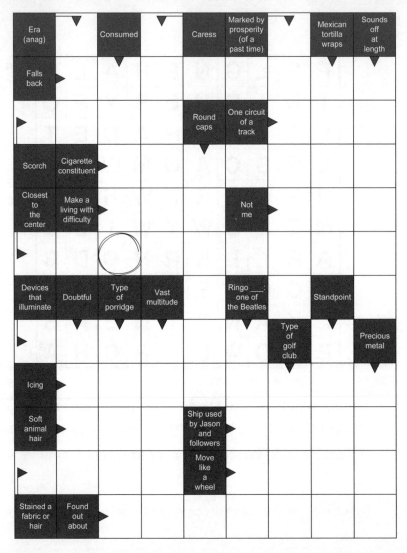

Era (anag)		Consumed		Caress	Marked by prosperity (of a past time)		Mexican tortilla wraps	Sounds off at length
Falls back								
				Round caps	One circuit of a track			
Scorch	Cigarette constituent							
Closest to the center	Make a living with difficulty				Not me			
Devices that illuminate	Doubtful	Type of porridge	Vast multitude		Ringo ___: one of the Beatles		Standpoint	
						Type of golf club		Precious metal
Icing								
Soft animal hair			Ship used by Jason and followers					
			Move like a wheel					
Stained a fabric or hair	Found out about							

PUZZLE SECTION

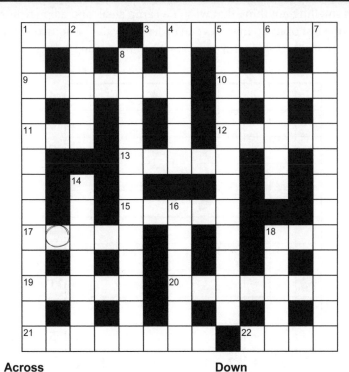

PUZZLE
31

Across

1 Slender freshwater fish (4)
3 Opera texts (8)
9 Devoted time to learning (7)
10 Small farm (5)
11 Moved quickly on foot (3)
12 A written document (5)
13 Upright (5)
15 Rude, impolite (5)
17 Solemn promises (5)
18 23rd Greek letter (3)
19 Declare invalid (5)
20 Giving the ball to another team member (7)
21 Boating (8)
22 Large group of people (4)

Down

1 Available for use as needed; optional (13)
2 Stir milk (5)
4 One of the halogens (6)
5 Person who receives office visitors (12)
6 Groups of actors (7)
7 Fascinatingly (13)
8 As quickly as possible (7-5)
14 Of great size (7)
16 Occur (6)
18 Cost (5)

THE BEEKEEPER'S HIVES

IRETURNED ONE LAST TIME to the scene of the crime, and my earlier suspicions were confirmed by a strong smell that hung around the orchard. Unfortunately, it had been a long day for Baskerville and he had no interest in smelling anything that wasn't a rump steak and a boney biscuit. But I had one last trick up my sleeve in order to locate the source of the smell. I was looking for the tree that was most visited by the angry bees.

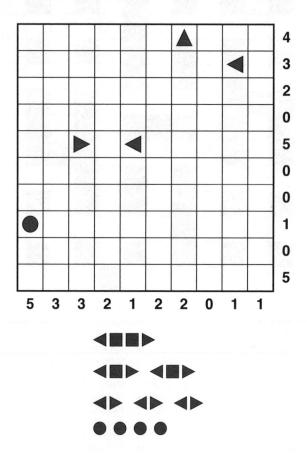

Find the location of the tree with the largest number of bees visiting.

THE BEEKEEPER'S HIVES

WELL, IT HAD BEEN QUITE A BUSY DAY, but before I could go home, it remained for me to note down for D.C. Copper everything I had discovered on my day's investigating.

KNOWNS AND UNKNOWNS

John the Beekeeper was allergic to bees.

☐ True ☐ Not true ☐ Unknown

Liza Liszt visited John on the day of his death.

☐ True ☐ Not true ☐ Unknown

The smell of an angry bee's pheromones is the same as rotten apples.

☐ True ☐ Not true ☐ Unknown

Frederick Bailey might have known of John's allergy.

☐ True ☐ Not true ☐ Unknown

Did you decode the message from *The Puzzleby Gazette*?

_ _ _ _   _ _ _ _   _ _ _ _ _ _

Write the name of your main suspect below:

CONCLUSION REACHED, I made my way to the police station, where D.C. Copper was just about to head home for the day. He paused, however, when he saw me and Baskerville making our way up the path.

"Have you figured it out, Miss Hemmingway?" he asked.

Which of these conclusions does Miss Hemmingway give?

1. It was a sad, but inevitable end for a beekeeper so allergic to bees. The queen had got stuck in the hive, and the bees, responding to her distress, had turned on poor John with fatal consequences.

2. The bees would never have attacked John if not encouraged to do so. Frederick Bailey, wishing to monopolize the sale of honey at the grocery store, had put in an unusually large order for bananas. These he hid in John's orchard, knowing the smell would drive the bees to fury and cause them to sting the beekeeper, with fatal consequences.

3. It was not bees that John was allergic to, but lemons. His niece Liza, perhaps after some inheritance of some sort, had left a bag of his old favourite sweets — lemon drops, and John had absent-mindedly eaten one, with fatal consequences.

ALL'S WELL THAT ENDS WELL — well, except for poor John, of course.

Grateful to be putting my feet up, I came back home and settled down to a new puzzle in the newsletter — this one thankfully free of encoded clues. Cat was purring happily across my shoulders, and a hungry Baskerville tucking into a hearty steak at my feet. I sipped my tea with a smile, happy in the knowledge that Puzzleby was safe and sound.

CASE TWO:

A

CRIME

OF POISSON

INTRODUCTION

ONE OF THE HIGHLIGHTS of the summer in Puzzleby is the annual fishing competition held at Lake Calamity. Local legend has it that a giant trout known as 'Calamity Jane' lurks in the depths, and, though she has not been seen for many years, her lure remains such that glory-seeking anglers from far and wide descend upon our sleepy village for a week each August in the hope of finally netting the 39 lb beauty—and the $500 top prize along with her.

It was on a particularly glorious late-summer's afternoon on the final day of this year's Lake Calamity Fish-Off that I found myself at the local pub, The Murdered Pint, enjoying a plum wine in the beer garden with Baskerville. I was just about to tackle this week's newsletter from Deirdre Dalliance when D.C. Copper burst into the beer garden, as white as a sheet.

"A body has been found on the bank of Lake Calamity!" he announced. "A fisherman, by the looks of it."

"No way!" exclaimed Billy Mead, the pub landlord. "Who is it, detective?"

"Must be one of the out-of-towners," replied D.C. Copper, squeezing onto a wooden picnic table. "I've never seen him before."

"How terribly sad," smirked Dahliah Dalliance from underneath a wide-brimmed sunhat, sipping on her Bloody Mary. "I've always had a soft spot for fishermen, although one did turn me down for dinner last week. But you know what they say—plenty more fish in the sea..."

At the mention of fish, D.C. Copper turned a fresh shade of gray, made his apologies and hurried off in such a fluster that he didn't even notice a stuffed envelope slide out from under his arm and land with a soft thud on the grass next to a less-than-impressed Baskerville.

"Butterfingers," I said under my breath, surreptitiously picking up the packet and dropping it into my wicker basket. "We should hold onto this, Baskerville. Anyone could come along and pick it up..."

A CRIME OF POISSON

LEFT TO MY OWN DEVICES with a glass of fruit wine and some puzzles to solve is precisely where I like to be. Having installed myself and Baskerville in a secluded and shady corner of the beer garden, I slid my finger along the lip of the envelope and gently tipped its contents onto the picnic table. The first thing to fall out was a registration card for the Lake Calamity Fish-Off, although it had been severely smudged and dirtied in the water. If I could only make out the registration number, I might be able to find out who the unfortunate fisherman was…

Solve the sudoku to find the victim's registration number.

PUZZLE 33

3		6						1
	2				1			
		9		6	7			4
	4	8						2
5						9	8	
9			8	1		3		
			5				9	
1						7		8

A CRIME OF POISSON

WITH THAT FIRST MYSTERY SUCCESSFULLY SOLVED, Baskerville and I made our way to the village square, where all the information about this year's Lake Calamity Fish-Off was displayed on the church noticeboard. On arrival, I observed that the letters and numbers on the bulletin board were all jumbled up—no doubt Father Featherby forgot to put his glasses on when he put up this year's rankings. Fortunately, I have never met a puzzle I didn't like, and I was able to decode the names of the contestants without too much trouble.

Use the numerology chart to figure out the names of the contestants.

PUZZLE
34

Numerology Chart

1	2	3	4	5	6	7	8	9
A	B	C	D	E	F	G	H	I
J	K	L	M	N	O	P	Q	R
S	T	U	V	W	X	Y	Z	

RANK	NAME	NATIONALITY	REGISTRATION NUMBER
1	M132 CH12T5RL57		813429567
2	14BR61E A2K9N165		448571089
3	11C835S BR6CH5T		692785413
4	33EM55T95E 36T26N		303682545
5	I9555 C62TO5		510398274

Write the name of the victim below:

_ _ _ _ _ _ / _ _ _ _ _ _ _ _

A CRIME OF POISSON

I MADE A NOTE OF THE NAME of the victim, along with the names of the other competitors (one never knows when such information might come in handy). I then reached carefully into the evidence packet D.C. Copper had so absent-mindedly dropped and retrieved a rather waterlogged wristwatch. The watch was clearly no longer working, and I would bet that it stopped when our unfortunate visitor entered the water. I may well have a clue to the victim's time of death right there in my hands! If only there wasn't so much dirty water obscuring the dial, I might be able to figure it out…

Use the completed sums to figure out the values of the shapes, then solve the remaining sums to find the time on the watch.

PUZZLE 35

$$\bullet \times \blacklozenge = 21$$

$$\blacktriangle + \bullet = 4$$

$$\blacksquare - \blacktriangle = 1$$

$$\blacklozenge - \blacklozenge =$$

$$\bullet - \blacksquare =$$

$$\blacksquare + \blacktriangle =$$

$$\blacktriangle \times \blacklozenge =$$

A CRIME OF POISSON

NOW THAT I KNEW WHAT TIME poor Monsieur Brochet went to his watery grave, that would certainly aid in my inquiries. But what on earth could have compelled him to be out on the lake in the small hours of the morning? Perhaps something else in this envelope would hold the answer. I reached in and extracted a rather soggy slip of paper. It appeared to have been torn out of the village newsletter, and whoever had done so had used one of the newsletter's excellent puzzles to send a message…

Solve the crossword then use the letters in the circles to solve the word scramble and decode the message.

PUZZLE
36

Across
1 Sample of cloth (6)
5 Position of employment (3)
7 Aqualung (5)
8 Contrary to (7)
9 Last Greek letter (5)
10 Country in Africa (8)
12 Break apart (6)
14 Side of an arch (6)
17 Rubbed with the hands (8)
18 Do really well at (5)
20 Belgian city (7)
21 Lose a contest intentionally (5)
22 Belonging to him (3)
23 Period of ten years (6)

Down
2 Pied ___ : bird (7)
3 Bring about using artifice (8)
4 Greek spirit (4)
5 Spear thrown in athletics (7)
6 Width (7)
7 Got to one's feet (5)
11 Recording device (8)
12 Big cat (7)
13 Draws forth (7)
15 Declare (anag) (7)
16 Brightly coloured parrot (5)
19 Engage in spirited fun (4)

_ _ _ _ / _ _ / _ _ _ / _ _ _ _ / _ _ / _ _ _ _ _ _ _

PUZZLE SECTION

PUZZLE 37

Epoch		Bolt for fastening metal plates		Arise from	Postponed		Indian lute	Packed carefully and neatly
Dreariness								
				Deprived of; lacking	Ignited			
Inheritor	Wavering vocal quality							
Meddle	First woman				Twist about a vertical axis			
Inside information (3-3)	Paul ___: former soccer player	Chimes	Exceed; perform better than		Frozen dew		Religious table	
						Poker stake		Cries
Impartial parties								
Feline				Upon				
				Pierce with a knife				
Clutched	Rosters (anag)							

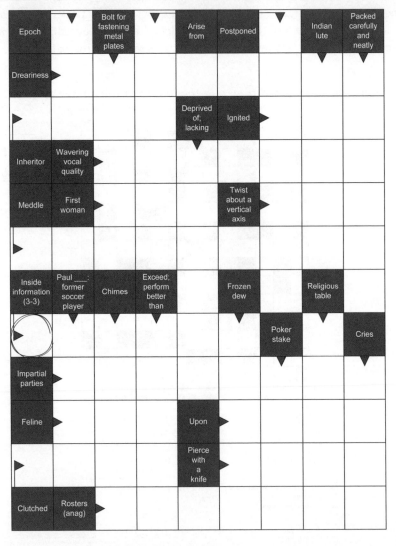

PUZZLE
38

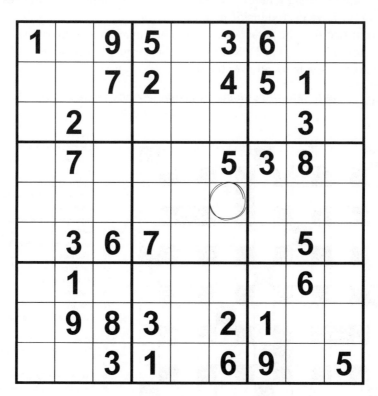

A Frenchman in London by Dahliah Dalliance

Miss Amy Dukes has vowed to hold any and all suitors up to her impeccable standards for a future husband. When Monsieur Timothée Depardieu joins her social circles, he turns her carefully curated world upside down. How is she to resist his charms, especially during the excitement of Mrs Sutton's diamonds going missing? Everyone's a suspect in this fantastique new book from Dahliah Dalliance!

A CRIME OF POISSON

IT CERTAINLY SEEMED AS THOUGH the time had come to pay a little visit to the police station. D.C. Copper smiled wryly when he saw me. "Ah, Miss Hemmingway, I did wonder when you would come by. I see you have my misplaced evidence."

"I brought it straight here," I said, sliding the envelope across the desk. "Well, I may have peered inside first..."

As it turned out, the detective was hunched over an account of the victim's toxicology report. Unfortunately, the coroner's pen had leaked and there were ink splotches all over the page.

PUZZLE 39

Complete the crossword, then use the circled letters to fill in the toxicology report.

Across
1 Engages in an argument (5)
4 Skin marks from wounds (5)
10 Remains (7)
11 Vacillate (5)
12 Small flashing dot on a radar screen (4)
13 Surrounded on all sides (8)
16 Banished (6)
17 Squirt a liquid in short bursts (6)
20 Infectious (8)
21 Clever remark (4)
23 Mark of repetition (5)
25 Irregularity (7)
26 Monastery church (5)
27 Eg Wordsworth and Keats (5)

Down
2 Person who expects the worst (9)
3 Travelled by horse (4)
5 Marsh marigolds (8)
6 Increase the running speed of an engine (3)
7 Multiply by three (6)
8 Existing (5)
9 Network of lines (4)
14 Incentive; substance like caffeine
15 Remove a monarch (8)
18 Current of air (6)
19 Go stealthily or furtively (5)
20 Closing section of music (4)
22 Extinct bird (4)
24 Bat (anag) (3)

Alcohol _____
Caffeine NEGATIVE
Nicotine NEGATIVE
Amphetamine NEGATIVE
Opiates NEGATIVE

A CRIME OF POISSON

MY, MY! It appears the unfortunate Monsieur Brochet was drinking like a fish before his untimely demise. Still, one would think that a fisherman ought to know better than to go for a midnight swim while intoxicated. Could there have been some foul play involved?

D.C. Copper seemed to read my mind, as he pointed me in the direction of a microscope. "These fibers were found around the drowned man's ankles. What do you think they are?"

Match the close-up to the fabric samples below to find out what kind of fibers were found on the body.

PUZZLE
40

linen   polyester   nylon   cotton

PUZZLEBY GAZETTE
VILLAGE NEWSLETTER

PUZZLE 41

```
R U T K C I T S E L D N A C Y
M A O O M Y I E C W E A P O N
S O N U R R A I N A P R U O B
O D O K S E S D E P O T W X R
S A I R W T M P R F R Z U T E
K G T G H S B J E B B Q E D N
F G C N I Y J S F A L J T Z N
F E U I T M S G E C C A Q J A
J R D P E O S N R H S O C U P
G E E I R Q S U S H H V C K S
O D D P T P S U S P E C T K S
Z R L D D S D L O G I C G X N
X U K A T B O A R D G A M E A
M M G E E V I T C E T E D T I
V M C L U E S T R A T E G Y L
```

BOARD GAME	DR BLACK	PROFESSOR PLUM
CANDLESTICK	LEAD PIPING	ROOM
CLU_S	LOGIC	ROPE
CROSS-REFERENCE	MRS PEACOCK	SPANNER
DAGGER	MRS WHITE	STRATEGY
DEDUCTION	MURDER	SUSPECT
DETECTIVE	MYSTERY	WEAPON

PUZZLE SECTION

PUZZLE 42

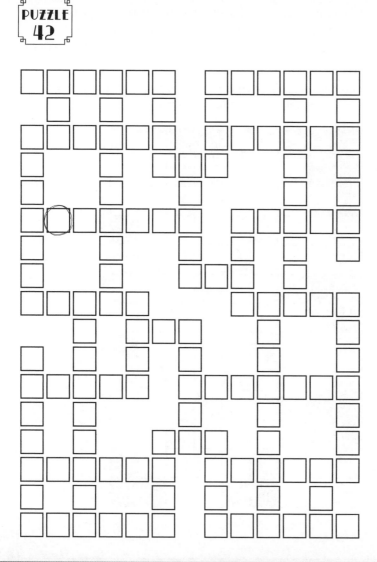

3 letters
Act
Ark
Chi
Ebb
The
Use

4 letters
Drub
Earn
Pair
Rose
Runs
Trio

5 letters
Basic
Epoch
Overs
Piste
Rapid
Steer

6 letters
Afloat
Bolero
Doused
Notate
Ocular
Skills
Unveil
Wander

7 letters
Coulomb
Dissent
Dollies
Impacts
Octopus
Squirts

9 letters
Autopilot
Dalliance
Effectual
Steamship

A CRIME OF POISSON

THE FIBERS FOUND AROUND HIS ANKLES are almost certainly evidence of a weight having been used to drown Monsieur Brochet. There could be no question now that we were looking at murder and I was well and truly on the hook. My list of competitors in the Lake Calamity Fish-Off had just become a list of my main suspects. Speaking of Lake Calamity, the time had come to visit the crime scene. Since the lake was so large, I asked D.C. Copper if he could point me to the exact location of the crime scene.

Solve the kakuro puzzle to find the coordinates of the crime scene in the circled boxes.

_ _ °N / _ _ _ °W

A CRIME OF POISSON

COORDINATES IN HAND, I went to leave the police station.

"Thank you for looking into this, Miss Hemmingway," began D.C. Copper. "I'd come with you, but I'm afraid I'm still feeling a little green around the gills."

Poor man—it takes a strong stomach to solve a murder.

"Fear not, detective – this slippery scoundrel won't slip through my net. Come, Baskerville," I said, rousing my faithful companion. "The game is on!"

Follow Baskerville through the village to the location of the coordinates.

38						86		
	40			77			100	94
	44		73	78		88		98
	35	46		79	82		91	
	23						67	
11	20		33				68		63
							61		57
	5		14	17			51		54
1			7		28				

PUZZLE 44

PUZZLEBY GAZETTE

VILLAGE NEWSLETTER

WHAT DO THE CARDS HOLD IN STORE FOR YOU?

Should you avoid salmon for the foreseeable future? Will you soon reel in a wife hook, line and sinker? Achillia Headland can tell your fortune for a small fee. Should you wish to be prepared for what lies ahead, enquire at 133 Wisteria Avenue for a discreet appointment.

9	4	6						
2			5					
8	7	4						
4			1	9				
	5			2				6
		2						
	1							

PUZZLE SECTION

PUZZLE 46

Court	Not on		Young male horses	Time periods	Denial of something	___ off: averted danger	Moved backwards	
			Follow on					
Small flower							Bluish green colour; duck	
			Variety of chalcedony					
Towards the stern	Coiffure		Rescuer					
Place where a wild animal lives		Small ornament		Seat (anag)				
				Lazy				
Pristine (5-3)		Seabirds		Refuse to admit		Repetition of a sound	Dense growth of trees	
								Sheltered side
Nobleman					Mountain pass			
					Weeding tool			
Symbol	Home for a pig				Lyric poem			

A CRIME OF POISSON

I FOLLOWED **BASKERVILLE** and the coordinates straight to the location of what I was now officially labeling a murder. Upon arrival at the taped-off crime scene, I let Baskerville off the lead and watched him paddle about in the cool water awhile. In the muddy grass around the spot where the body was found, I observed two sets of footprints. One set surely matched D.C. Copper's police-issued boots, but which one?

Match the two sets of footprints to the correct type of shoe.

PUZZLE 47

1: Work Boots

2: Wellington Boots

3: D.C. Copper

4: Policeman's shoes

5: Work Boots

6: Farmer's Boots

7. Oxford Brogues

8. Slippers

A CRIME OF POISSON

HAVING ELIMINATED **D.C. COPPER'S FOOTPRINTS** from my inquiries, it seemed like the most logical thing to do was to follow the second, mysterious set of prints and see where they took us. I summoned Baskerville (after all, what's the use of having an old blood hound if you can't occasionally use him to sniff out a murderer?) and set him on the trail.

Guide Baskerville as he makes his way through the muddy maze to see where the footprints lead.

START

PUZZLE
48

FINISH

PUZZLE SECTION

PUZZLE 49

15	18	25	18	19	■	9	17	14	14	3	11	6
16	■	18	■	13	■	3	■	■	12	■	18	■
12	■	8	■	3	■	11	■	9	19	12	24	2
19	17	10	1	15	13	10	1	■	6	■	17	■
18	■	12	■	3	■	18	■	26	12	17	15	7
8	17	21	3	11	13	19	2	■	7	■	■	18
3	■	18	■	15	■	■	15	■	15	■	■	10
11	■	■	13	■	10	16	17	7	5	9	13	16
18	23	13	20	18	■	12	■	3	■	17	■	11
■	13	■	17	■	10	12	11	14	18	7	7	3
13	6	3	8	18	■	19	■	14	■	7	■	22
■	17	■	7	■	■	13	■	18	■	18	■	17
4	18	13	15	7	8	2	■	11	17	19	15	18

A B C D E F G H I J K L M N O P Q R S T U V W X Y Z

1	2	3	4	5	6	7	8	9	10	11	12	13
										N		A

14	15	16	17	18	19	20	21	22	23	24	25	26
F												

PUZZLEBY GAZETTE
VILLAGE NEWSLETTER

PUZZLE
50

	3				5		7	
4				1		9		8
			4				6	
						5		
	9		8	6	2		4	
		1						
	5				9			
2		8		3				6
	7		2				5	

A CRIME OF POISSON

THE FOOTPRINTS LED US TO THE ROAD, then disappeared. Drat. The killer must have escaped in a vehicle. At that moment, I spotted Ambrose Atkinson waving us over from her holiday cottage on the other side of the road.

"Please hurry up and solve this murder so that we can finish the competition," began Ambrose. "I couldn't stand seeing Mack Chatterley take the crown again, and I believe in my chances this year."

"You might be able to help me, Ambrose," I replied. "I don't suppose you spotted any cars on this road in the early hours of this morning?"

"As a matter of fact, I did," Ambrose replied, pulling a piece of paper from her pocket. "I was woken up by a very noisy sports car, and I jotted down the license plate number so that I could hunt them down this morning and give them a piece of my mind. It was very dark, so I'm afraid I didn't get the whole thing, mind you…"

PUZZLE 51

Complete the codebreaker and use the letters in the circles to complete the license plate.

_ _ 9 6 _ _ _

A B C D E F G H I J K L M N O P Q R S T U V W X Y Z

1	2	3	4	5	6	7	8	9	10	11	12	13
		M									J	

14	15	16	17	18	19	20	21	22	23	24	25	26
											K	

A CRIME OF POISSON

THIS WAS INDEED A BREAKTHROUGH. I knew that there were four people in the village who owned an car matching Ambrose's description. Using my keen intellect, I was sure I could narrow down the possible drivers spotted leaving the scene of the crime.

Use these statements to establish who Ambrose might have seen.

> My license plate has only consonants.

IRENE COTTON

> My license plate has a prime number.

FATHER FEATHERBY

> My license plate has no multiples of 3.

BILLY MEAD

> My license plate is in alphabetical order.

MACK CHATTERLEY

Which two people could the vehicle belong to?

_____ and _____

PUZZLEBY GAZETTE

VILLAGE NEWSLETTER

PUZZLE SECTION

PUZZLE 53

A	E	K	Y	P	T	Y	R	C	M	A	Y	A	A	G
R	E	E	E	F	L	L	J	S	O	A	G	S	C	R
A	L	L	S	Y	Q	H	A	L	I	B	U	T	O	S
H	O	P	H	T	U	O	M	L	E	S	I	H	C	X
C	S	F	S	H	B	U	R	O	L	E	T	A	I	W
C	N	I	I	L	M	E	O	S	O	P	A	G	N	X
I	I	S	F	R	W	A	U	E	S	A	R	F	E	D
T	F	H	K	E	T	E	C	L	D	L	F	I	R	T
C	L	L	C	G	P	R	N	K	A	R	I	S	O	T
R	R	L	O	U	T	I	O	M	E	C	S	H	L	H
A	U	I	R	U	Z	C	P	U	H	R	H	N	K	S
Z	C	R	R	R	N	R	J	Y	T	S	E	O	A	O
I	T	B	R	R	E	D	R	T	A	U	S	L	N	Y
G	O	B	Y	Y	D	R	E	U	L	B	I	T	C	Y
T	B	G	R	O	U	P	E	R	F	B	X	O	S	A

ARCTIC CHAR	EULACHON	HALIBUT
BAY PIPEFISH	FLATHEAD SOLE	KELPFISH
BRILL	FLOUNDER	LAMPREY
CHISELMOUTH	GOBY	MACKEREL
COBIA	GROUPER	ROCKFISH
COCI_ERO	GUITARFISH	TROUT
CURLFIN SOLE	HAGFISH	TURBOT

PUZZLEBY GAZETTE
VILLAGE NEWSLETTER

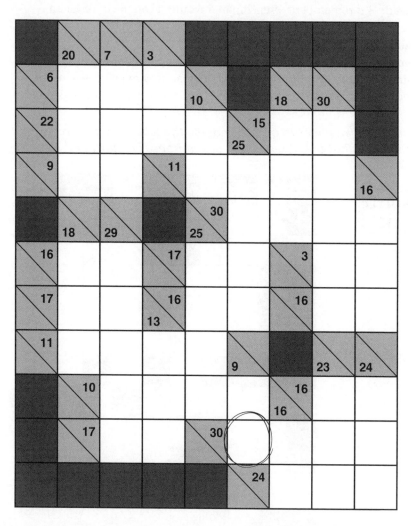

A CRIME OF POISSON

I DECIDED TO RETURN TO THE VILLAGE and drop by The Murdered Pint to see if anyone remembered our ill-fated Frenchman having partaken of a drink or six the previous night.

"Not in 'ere, Miss Hemmingway," replied the ruddy-faced landlord, Billy Mead. "I'd remember a Frenchman, I would. I can never resist an opportunity to practice me French."

I sighed, disappointed. Another dead end.

"Somethin' odd did 'appen 'ere last night though," continued Billy, scratching his chin thoughtfully. "We 'ad a break-in. I'm just checkin' the inventory now to see what was stolen. Perhaps you can help me make sense of it?"

Solve the arrow words puzzle and use the letters in the circles to discover what two things were stolen from The Murdered Pint.

**PUZZLE
55**

Era (anag)		Consumed		Caress	Marked by prosperity (of a past time)		Mexican tortilla wraps	Sounds off at length
Falls back								
				Round caps	One circuit of a track			
Scorch	Cigarette constituent							
Closest to the castle	Make a living with difficulty				Not me			
Devices that illuminate	Doubtful	Type of porridge	Vast multitude		Ringo ___, one of the Beatles		Standpoint	
						Type of golf club		Precious metal
Icing								
Soft animal hair			Ship used by Jason and followers					
			Move like a wheel					
Stained a fabric or hair	Found out about							

Write the stolen items below:

_ _ _ and _ _ _

A CRIME OF POISSON

IT WAS THEN THAT **I** REMEMBERED that the two Welsh sisters, Irene and Clementine Cotton were staying in a room above The Murdered Pint for the duration of the Lake Calamity Fish-Off. I asked Billy if I might have a word with them.

"I can't see why not, Miss Hemmingway," replied Billy. "But first, I don't s'pose you've got your fingerprint dusting kit on you, do you?" He pointed at the broken padlock, which was covered in inky fingerprints.

Luckily, like any self-respecting sleuth, I keep a fingerprint dusting kit on me at all times.

"Don't worry, Billy, we'll catch this sticky-fingered thief in no time," I assured the landlord.

"Mercy boo-coups, Miss Hemmingway!" chimed Billy.

Match the fingerprints pulled from the padlock to the possible suspects.

PUZZLE
56

Billy Mead

Clementine Cotton

Irene Cotton

Mack Chatterley

Ambrose Atkinson

Jacques Brochet

PUZZLE 57

YOUR HOROSCOPE
FROM ACHILLIA
HEADLAND

This week, your passion and fervor are admirable. You will be keen to impress those around you—but beware! Pride often comes before a fall. Saturn and Pluto are in conjunction, a phenomenon that often heralds a global shift. Something will happen that affects multiple places—do you want to be in the heart and sole [sic] of it all?

		5		6	7	1		3
1					3	7	8	
7			1	8				
			○	9			5	1
	1						3	
9		8		3				
				2	6			7
	2	4	3					9
5		7	9	1		3		

PUZZLE SECTION

PUZZLE
58

Across

1 Decays (4)
3 Leonardo ___ : Romeo + Juliet actor (8)
9 Large spotted cat (7)
10 Out of fashion (5)
11 Spring flower (5)
12 A parent's mother (7)
13 One's twilight years (3,3)
15 Majestic; wonderful (6)
17 Seasoned pork sausage (7)
18 George ___ : Middlemarch writer (5)
20 Type of chemical bond (5)
21 River in South America (7)
22 Splashing with water (8)
23 Poses a question (4)

Down

1 Connections or associations (13)
2 Mythical monster (5)
4 Deep blue color (6)
5 Using letters and numbers (12)
6 Remains (7)
7 Excessively striving (13)
8 Carefree (5-2-5)
14 One who finds water by dowsing (7)
16 Wealthy person in business (6)
19 People who are greatly admired (5)

A CRIME OF POISSON

IMADE MY WAY UP TO THE ROOMS above The Murdered Pint, but it was only when I reached the top of the stairs that I realized Billy hadn't told me which room the Cotton sisters were staying in. I knew I could go back downstairs and ask him, but poor old Baskerville looked like another trip up and down the stairs might just do him in, and I had quite enough dead bodies on my plate for one day, thank you very much. Regardless, I was certain I could work it out for myself.

Solve the puzzle to find out which room the Cotton sisters are staying in.

1) The door number is an odd number.
2) The door number is not a prime number.
3) The door number is a multiple of three.
4) The door number is not a square number.

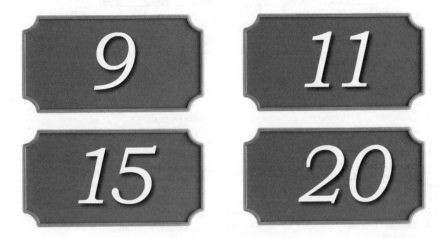

A CRIME OF POISSON

IKNOCKED ON THE DOOR AND THE TALL, elegant Clementine Cotton answered and invited me inside. Her sister, Irene poured us some tea while Clementine made a fuss of Baskerville.

"Are you here about Jacques' notebook?" asked Irene.

"Yes," I lied without hesitation, sensing an unexpected breakthrough. Irene reached under the sagging sofa and retrieved a leatherbound notebook with a small, two-digit lock.

"We took it from his bag at the lake yesterday. We thought we might be able to use it to figure out the secret to his success, but we can't crack the code," she explained.

"We feel awful about it now, of course," Clementine finished, sheepishly.

Well, I was stumped. Rather than fumbling around trying to guess the code, I decided to give my brain a little break and peruse the newsletter puzzle pages while I sipped my tea. One riddle in particular caught my eye— would it help me find the code to unlock the padlock?

Solve the riddle to unlock the diary.

PUZZLE
60

10 fish are in a tank.

2 fish drown.
4 fish swim away.
3 fish die.

How many are there now?

_____

PUZZLE 61

	1			◯					31
3		8		17	27	38	37	33	
4	9					40			
	12	19			43	44			
							76	48	
	23	71	92		82		79		
			95						
67		97	98					57	51
	68		100	88		85			
		63			60				53

84

PUZZLEBY GAZETTE
VILLAGE NEWSLETTER

PUZZLE
62

	I			G		A		S	
C	O	R	E	A		R	E	G	A	I	N
	I				A		○			
U	N		A	P		O	I	N	T	S
	L		R	E		C		I	
L	I	U	I	D	S		S		P		R
		N		S		I		L		T
S	P	I	T	E		N		T		H
	A		S		S		U	
L	I	R	E	T	T	I		R	E	E
	C		I		E		I	
	L	L	I	P		H	O	S	T	E	L
	Y		S		T		T		R

A B C D E F G H I J K L M N O P Q R S T U V W X Y Z

85

A CRIME OF POISSON

WITH THE CODE TO MONSIEUR BROCHET'S NOTEBOOK CRACKED, the scales had certainly tipped in my favor. Of course, it was all written in French, but thanks to my summers spent with Aunt Odette in Versailles, I was able to translate it quite elegantly, if I say so myself. On the first page, Monsieur Brochet had listed each fish that he had caught during that year's competition. Alas, it appeared the enigmatic Monsieur Brochet went to great lengths to protect his fishing secrets and had written the names of the fish in code. I do believe we would have got along rather well.

Solve the word scrambles to discover the types of fish
Monsieur Brochet caught.

PUZZLE 63			
IKPE	_ _ _ _	3 lb
RCPA	_ _ _ _	__ lb
EPHCR	_ _ _ _ _	__ lb
OTTUR	_ _ _ _ _	__ lb
ARHOC	_ _ _ _ _	__ lb
FCIHAST	_ _ _ _ _ _ _	6 lb

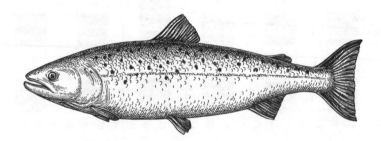

A CRIME OF POISSON

NEXT TO EACH FISH, Monsieur Brochet had jotted down its weight (in very nice handwriting, I might add). However, some of the weights had been obscured by pesky water droplets.

Solve the jigsaw sudoku to find the missing weights of the fish in the grey boxes, then fill them in on the previous page.

PUZZLE 64

	8	6	5					3
			4	2				8
						1		
		1	3			2	4	
			6				5	
							1	
	2							
				9				
					4			

PUZZLEBY GAZETTE

VILLAGE NEWSLETTER

PUZZLE 65

A B C D E F G H I J K L M N O P Q R S T U V W X Y Z

PUZZLE SECTION

PUZZLE 66

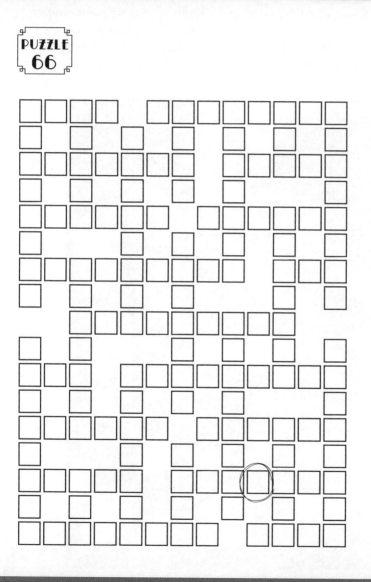

3 letters
Boa
Emu
Ill
Vat

4 letters
Bevy
Play
Spar
Tutu

5 letters
Altar
Azure
Delta
Table

6 letters
Serial
Tariff
Uptake
Wields

7 letters
Couture
Entrant
Involve
Mediate
Perturb
Reddens
Vinegar

8 letters
Assembly
Calamari
Graffiti
Pheasant
Reassert
Seawater
Slippery
Stamping

9 letters
Nectarine
Readiness
Universal

A CRIME OF POISSON

WITH MY LIST OF SUSPECTS DWINDLING, it seemed like a good moment to visit the defending champion of the Lake Calamity Fish-Off. Since Mack Chatterley owned the local fish and chip shop, Final Resting Plaice, it was also the perfect opportunity to pick up some supper for myself, Baskerville and, of course, Cat, who would never forgive me otherwise. Upon my arrival at Final Resting Plaice, however, my eagle eyes could immediately tell that there had been some changes since the last time I had visited.

A CRIME OF POISSON

Spot the six differences between the two pictures.

PUZZLE
67

PUZZLEBY GAZETTE
VILLAGE NEWSLETTER

PUZZLE
68

A	M	H	A	I	G	D	E	S	E
U	A	S	I	L	A	W	A	A	T
S	H	D	N	V	L	D	R	M	R
T	R	E	O	E	A	S	S	L	E
I	I	S	T	R	R	A	E	E	C
N	L	P	M	A	N	W	O	R	U
S	T	A	X	W	E	W	H	T	R
U	I	T	R	A	T	A	R	K	B
C	A	M	I	L	S	T	T	O	C
H	E	T	H	L	O	W	E	N	S

Newsreaders

Alagiah, Austin, Bruce, Derham, Edwards, Esler, Hill, Maitlis, Mates, Owen, Paxman, Raw_rth, Scott, Silverton, Stewart, Suchet, Wark

PUZZLE 69

21	7	26	22	3	10		10	21	21	13	21	9
9		16		9		3		3		22		21
10	21	11	8	22	10	26		26		23		6
2		16		21		16	24	22	17	22	10	21
7	22	12	21	9		9		17				2
1		9				21		4	2	10	2	11
		2		20	22	16	11	2		18		
9	15	19	14	2		12				15		6
22				9		9		14	9	22	14	21
6	21	7	15	4	22	2		22		9		9
6		23		22		6	25	5	2	19	2	10
21		22		10		26		16		21		16
17	22	4	12	26	25		14	15	9	17	21	4

A B C D E F G H I J K L M N O P Q R S T U V W X Y Z

1	2	3	4	5	6	7	8	9	10	11	12	13
							F					K

14	15	16	17	18	19	20	21	22	23	24	25	26
								I				

A CRIME OF POISSON

MACK WAS CLEARLY IN NO MOOD TO CHITCHAT; he served me and rushed me out of the place so quickly I could barely catch my breath! Back home, I received a far warmer welcome from Cat who was most pleased to see me (although I suspect he was more pleased to see his supper). As I extracted Cat's fish from the bag, I noticed that it had been wrapped in pages from last week's Puzzleby newsletter. I smoothed out the pages, keen to see if there were any old puzzles I hadn't yet completed, when one article caught my eye. It appeared that it had caught Mack's eye too, as he had circled some of the letters on the page…

*Use the circled letters to solve
the word scramble below.*

… preparing to compete in this year's acclaimed Lake Calamity Fish-Off. Today, I had the pleasure of sitting down with newcomer, Jacques Brochet, who has traveled all the way from France for the chance to net a win.

Welcome to Puzzleby, Monsieur Brochet. Why did you decide to take part in this year's competition?

"I read an article about the fish you call Calamity Jane last year and I was intrigued. I could not believe that no one had been successful in catching her. I decided then that I would travel to your village and take part in the competition, I could not resist."

The reigning champion is a Puzzleby local. Do you think you stand a chance against him?

"I am sure he is a very gifted fisherman, but I am here to win. I will be the one to catch Calamity Jane once and for all."

Well, you heard it here first! We will certainly be watching the events of this year's competition unfold with heightened interest, it's sure to be a fierce competition…

_ _ _ _ / _ _ _ _ _ / _ _ _ _ _ / _ _ _ _

A CRIME OF POISSON

WELL, I SAY! THIS WAS ALL RATHER FISHY. It seemed as though our poor Monsieur Brochet had certainly put a target on his back in his short time in Puzzleby, but I still couldn't be sure that I had a proper grasp on the murderer's motive. There was nothing else to do but put my slippers on, polish off my supper, and relax with some puzzles. Perhaps the crossword contained the answer at the heart of this fishy case.

Solve the crossword to find another clue.

PUZZLE
71

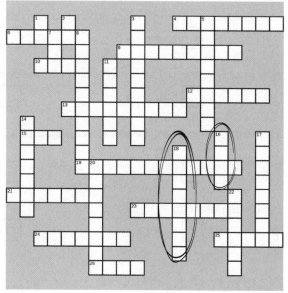

Across

4 Extremely difficult (8)

6 Characteristic of the universe (6)

9 The act of altering clothing to fit (9)

10 Headwear, attached to a garment (4)

12 To quit (4,2)

13 Rival university to Oxford (9)

15 Mascot of Derby County Football Club (3)

19 The act of checking a text for errors (12)

21 David _____, Author of The Belgariad (7)

23 Site of the world's first water-powered cotton mill (8)

24 Weepy (7)

25 Patrick _____, singer in the band Fall Out Boy (5)

26 Catherine ____ Jones, Welsh actress (4)

Down

1 While (2)

2 Milwaukee's state (abbreviation) (2)

3 Smooth coffee with steamed milk (4,5)

5 Improving the mind; enlightening (8)

7 Noise made by a cow (3)

8 Hogwash (10)

11 The eldest son of Israel, according to the book of Genesis (6)

14 Andalusian home of the Alhambra (7)

16 Companion of Tarzan (4)

17 Indulge in fantasy (8)

18 Misfortune or disaster (8)

20 Detective in the TV show Brooklyn Nine Nine (4,4)

22 Project manager of a book (6)

A CRIME OF POISSON

THOUGHTS WHIRLING, I sat back in my chair and frowned as I thought over everything I had discovered. My trusty pen and notebook were employed in which to scribble down my thoughts...

KNOWNS AND UNKNOWNS

Clementine and Irene Cotton read Jacques Brochet's notebook.

☐ True ☐ Not true ☐ Unknown

Mack Chatterley's car was spotted leaving the scene of the crime.

☐ True ☐ Not true ☐ Unknown

Billy Mead saw Jacques Brochet at The Murdered Pint on the night of his death.

☐ True ☐ Not true ☐ Unknown

Jacques Brochet could not swim.

☐ True ☐ Not true ☐ Unknown

Did you decode the message from *The Puzzleby Gazette*?

___   _____   _____

Write the name of your main suspect below:

A CRIME OF POISSON

THAT WAS THE FINAL NAIL IN THE COFFIN, if you'll pardon the pun. I kicked off my slippers, gathered my notes and summoned Baskerville. We made our way through the village to the police station, where D.C. Copper was just locking up for the day.

"Ah, Miss Hemmingway," he called. "Did you manage to get to the bottom of Monsieur Brochet's death?"

Which of these conclusions does Miss Hemmingway give?

1. Jacques Brochet, having been unsuccessful in fulfilling his promise of catching Calamity Jane, stole two bottles of rum from The Murdered Pint. He overindulged and ended up falling into Lake Calamity, getting tangled in his own fishing net and drowning himself along with his sorrows. It was a tragic accident and a sad end for the visiting Frenchman.

2. Having been woken in the night, Ambrose Atkinson spotted Jacques Brochet going for a late-night fishing session and decided to follow him. At Lake Calamity, Ambrose hid in the bushes to see what she could learn about Jacques' fishing techniques. While she was watching, she saw Billy Mead hit Jacques over the head with an oar. Billy then stole Jacques' notebook and fled the scene on foot while Jacques stumbled into the lake and drowned.

3. Mack Chatterley lured Jacques Brochet to the lake, possibly under the guise of congratulating him for having finally caught Calamity Jane, and Jacques had fallen for it, hook, line and sinker. Mack proceeded to get Jacques drunk on the rum he had stolen from The Murdered Pint, and pushed the Frenchman into Lake Calamity with the doorstop from Final Resting Plaice tied to his ankles. Mack then took Calamity Jane for himself, keeping her fresh using the ice he also stole from the pub so that he could pretend to have caught her the following day and retain his crown as champion of the Lake Calamity Fish-Off.

CASE THREE:

A

FATEFUL

FESTIVAL

INTRODUCTION

IT WAS A LOVELY SUNNY DAY IN THE VILLAGE; the perfect weather for the annual summer festival, which was taking place outside the church.

I was at the mailbox, sending a letter to *The Puzzleby Gazette*'s opinion page about the wonderful puzzles they had been featuring lately (and please could you make some of them more challenging?).

Just then, Brett the Baker's Boy rushed past on his way to the surgery. "Mrs Elstree needs help!" he cried. "She's just collapsed in the judging tent!"

Paula Elstree, I knew, often judged the baking competition at the gala, much to the village's delight. How tragic that she had been taken ill!

"Maybe the tent was too hot?" I wondered aloud to Baskerville, who was sniffing around a nearby lamppost, and Cat, preening in the sun.

"Last year," said Dahliah Dalliance, who was just passing by the mailbox, "Paula had a terrible reaction because one of the shortbread slices contained peanuts. Not that I'd ever let her try my baking again after what she said about my last book—I bet she didn't even read it!"

I decided not to say that I hadn't yet read Dahliah's latest novel either, and instead turned towards the church. I was on my way to the festival anyway; I like the decorations and the local produce. My faithful companions and I hurried down to see what was going on. Unfortunately, Paula Elstree had already been pronounced dead at the scene...

A FATEFUL FESTIVAL

PAULA WAS ALLERGIC TO PEANUTS! Could her death be merely a tragic accident, I wondered. I knew I had to start by deducing the fatal cake's ingredients to see if there was anything amiss, but the recipe that each contestant had to follow was hard to read; a jumble of letters that I had to strain even my keen eyes to understand…

There are eleven ingredients in the word search below. Complete the puzzle to see if the cake contained anything that could have triggered an allergic reaction in Paula.

PUZZLE
72

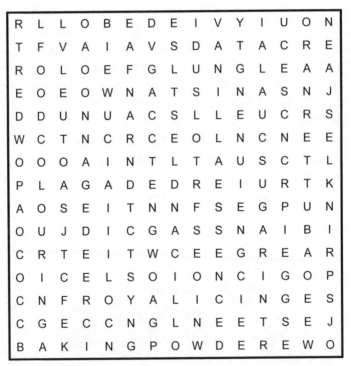

R	L	L	O	B	E	D	E	I	V	Y	I	U	O	N
T	F	V	A	I	A	V	S	D	A	T	A	C	R	E
R	O	L	O	E	F	G	L	U	N	G	L	E	A	A
E	O	E	O	W	N	A	T	S	I	N	A	S	N	J
D	D	U	N	U	A	C	S	L	L	E	U	C	R	S
W	C	T	N	C	R	C	E	O	L	N	C	N	E	E
O	O	O	A	I	N	T	L	T	A	U	S	C	T	L
P	L	A	G	A	D	E	D	R	E	I	U	R	T	K
A	O	S	E	I	T	N	N	F	S	E	G	P	U	N
O	U	J	D	I	C	G	A	S	S	N	A	I	B	I
C	R	T	E	I	T	W	C	E	E	G	R	E	A	R
O	I	C	E	L	S	O	I	O	N	C	I	G	O	P
C	N	F	R	O	Y	A	L	I	C	I	N	G	E	S
C	G	E	C	C	N	G	L	N	E	E	T	S	E	J
B	A	K	I	N	G	P	O	W	D	E	R	E	W	O

A FATEFUL FESTIVAL

PERHAPS THEN, SOMETHING ELSE was the cause of Miss Elstree's demise. But what? My mind whirled with possibilities, and I wondered whether that morning's puzzle would be of use in freeing my mind from its turmoil—but wait! Some of the squares were highlighted. Could a clue be lying within?

Solve the arrow word and unscramble the word it reveals.

PUZZLE 73

Mature people		Group of birds		Kind or sort		Command		Reduce the volume
Disordered state of mind								
Flashed on and off at speed		Ancient				Type of perfume (4,5)		Document of ownership
Small viper		Pull out a hair		Repetition to aid memory				
			For a short time		Observe			
Oppress grievously	Harsh and grating in sound		Harsh and serious in manner		Finish			
				Block a decision		Bathroom mineral powder	_____ Fitzgerald: famous jazz singer
Switch on							
Emaciated							
Blue-green colour		Narrate a story once again					
				Killer whale			

PUZZLEBY GAZETTE
VILLAGE NEWSLETTER

PUZZLE
74

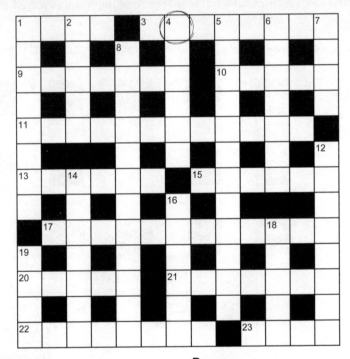

Across

1 Lie in ambush (4)
3 Religious deserter (8)
9 Two-wheeled vehicle (7)
10 Expels from a position (5)
11 The proprietor of an eating establishment (12)
13 Calamitous (6)
15 Cold season (6)
17 Comical tuner (anag) (12)
20 Regal (5)
21 Existing at the beginning (7)
22 All people (8)
23 Jelly or culture medium (4)

Down

1 Set free (8)
2 Moves back and forth (5)
4 Metrical writing (6)
5 Malfunction or fail (of an electrical device) (5-7)
6 Attack (7)
7 Compass point (4)
8 Now and then (12)
12 Tooth (8)
14 Assistant (7)
16 Vast number of people (6)
18 Chopping (5)
19 Sea eagle (4)

PUZZLEBY GAZETTE

VILLAGE NEWSLETTER

PUZZLE SECTION

PUZZLE 75

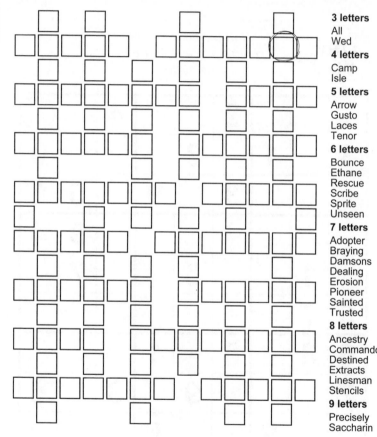

3 letters
All
Wed

4 letters
Camp
Isle

5 letters
Arrow
Gusto
Laces
Tenor

6 letters
Bounce
Ethane
Rescue
Scribe
Sprite
Unseen

7 letters
Adopter
Braying
Damsons
Dealing
Erosion
Pioneer
Sainted
Trusted

8 letters
Ancestry
Commando
Destined
Extracts
Linesman
Stencils

9 letters
Precisely
Saccharin

A FATEFUL FESTIVAL

HOME BREWING ASIDE, there was only one place in the village to find such things, but when I reached the pharmacy, I found myself locked out once again. There was a sudoku puzzle taped to the door. Could that hold the code for the new lock?

PUZZLE
76

Find the code for the pharmacy lock hidden in the sudoku.

		◯	2			4		◯
3		1		8				9
			3		9		5	1
				◯			9	4
	1			5			7	
5	7			◯				
6	8		5		1			
7				9		3		6
		9			6			

A FATEFUL FESTIVAL

THE **SHELVES INSIDE HAD BEEN RANSACKED** and there were footprints coming from a pile of powder on the floor. They led out of the back door and round the corner, where the trail faded. Not to be deterred, my trusty hound (with a bit of coaxing) picked up the scent.

"Good boy, Baskerville!" I cried. Cat and I followed his meandering path around the village until we arrived at a pretty little thatched cottage on the outskirts of town.

Solve the king's journey to help Baskerville follow the footprints.

PUZZLE 77

	50					85			
		54		76				100	99
			72			88	95		
	56					82		92	
45			68	69	79	80	1		
			64			38	2		
29		59	61	62				8	6
			41			35	18		
	27		32					14	
25				21					12

105

PUZZLE 78

6				7				
2	3	5		6				
8				2		1		
4		3						
	9		7			2		
					3			9
	6		5					7
			9		2	4	3	
		4						8

PUZZLE
79

Across

1 Consider to be true (6)
5 Young bear (3)
7 Yellow-orange pigment (5)
8 Sedentary (7)
9 Remains expectantly (5)
10 Stole; grabbed suddenly (8)
12 Active; energetic (6)
14 Wolfgang ___ : Austrian
composer (6)
17 Supplemental part of a book (8)
18 Artifice (5)
20 Pay homage to (7)
21 Labor organisation (5)
22 Eg water vapour (3)
23 Strangest (6)

Down

2 Italian red wine (7)
3 Lavish (8)
4 Exclamation of relief (4)
5 Mark written under a letter (7)
6 Beetroot soup (7)
7 Unpleasant giants (5)
11 In poor condition (3-5)
12 Allowing (7)
13 More than one (7)
15 Dried grapes (7)
16 Produce eggs (5)
19 Make a garment using wool (4)

A FATEFUL FESTIVAL

I SLIPPED THROUGH THE GARDEN GATE, but Baskerville was not yet finished with his trail. He led me round and round the herb garden, sniffing at every stone and garden gnome, until we came to a plant that looked out of place amongst its companions in the flowerbed. Frowning, I bent down to inspect it in closer detail.

Which plant is not listed in the pathfinder?

PUZZLE
80

L	A	L	L	I	D	M	A	D	R
L	I	C	E	G	M	O	V	E	A
S	P	L	R	A	C	H	I	S	C
J	C	I	A	D	H	A	M	O	R
A	O	R	R	I	S	R	E	S	E
S	H	S	E	E	L	Y	F	Y	M
M	S	S	A	M	L	N	E	H	T
I	E	G	R	O	E	N	M	A	R
N	R	A	G	N	T	M	M	A	O
E	O	N	O	N	U	E	G	R	J

Allspice, Belladonna, Cardamom, Chives, Dill, Fennel, Garlic, Horseradish, Jasmine, Lemongrass, Marjoram, Nutmeg, Oregano, Rosemary, Thyme

A FATEFUL FESTIVAL

WHAT ON EARTH IS THAT DOING IN AN HERB GARDEN?

I wondered, before jerking sharply on the leash and pulling my canine companion back.

"Careful, Baskerville - don't touch that!" I warned. The old hound huffed, but came to sit obediently at my feet.

I glanced down to pat him and give him a biscuit as a reward, when I noticed a scrap of paper lying in the grass - a piece torn from a lined notepad. Curious, I picked it up and discovered a riddle scrawled across the paper. Perhaps this could tell me why the garden had been replanted? Pulling my coat a little tighter against the chill of the evening, I set about solving the strange riddle.

Can you solve the riddle?

> PUZZLE
> 81

A serial killer kidnapped three men and three women. He gave each one of them two pills and a glass of water. He ordered them to take one pill, telling them that one was poisonous and the other was harmless. He promised that whichever pill the victim did not take, he would swallow himself. Each captive took a pill, and each one of them died. How did the serial killer get them all to take the poison?

PUZZLEBY GAZETTE
VILLAGE NEWSLETTER

PUZZLE
82

A B C D E F G H I J K L M N O P Q R S T U V W X Y Z

Choux Buns and Cyanide, by Dahliah Dalliance

Miss Tamsin Shooter has been preparing for Duffield's Baking Show ever since her mama let her hold a rolling pin. There's no cake she can't bake, and she plans to she plans to wow the judges with her infamous raspberry and almond Bakewell cake. Unfortunately, her rival, Miss Evelyn Barker, plans to make the same dish, and with the attentions of Chef Ezra Davidson up for grabs, there's nothing they won't do to win.

The delicious new thriller from Dahliah Dalliance, out now.

PUZZLE 83

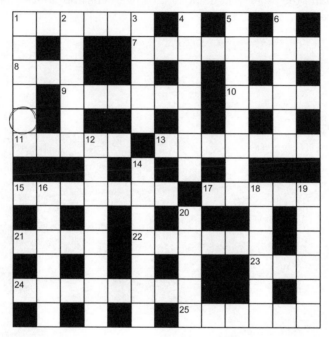

Across

1 Movable helmet parts (6)
7 Reaction (anag) (8)
8 Long period of time (3)
9 Recount (6)
10 Unattractive (4)
11 Crime of burning something (5)
13 Excavating machines (7)
15 Motorcycle attachment (7)
17 Sudden movements (5)
21 Freezes over (4)
22 Moved up and down on water (6)
23 Annoy (3)
24 Greatly impress (8)
25 Sailing vessels (6)

Down

1 Capital of Austria (6)
2 Fiery particles (6)
3 Discard; throw away (5)
4 Book of the Bible (7)
5 Strive (8)
6 US monetary unit (6)
12 ___ one's welcome: remain for too long (8)
14 River in Africa (7)
16 Units of linear measure (6)
18 Swollen edible root (6)
19 Cooks in wood chippings (6)
20 Monastery church (5)

A FATEFUL FESTIVAL

THERE WAS SOMETHING ELSE AMISS HERE. This garden had been named one of the village's best only a few weeks ago, and I had toured it with the parish council as they explained their decision. Now, I looked around the otherwise-meticulous flowerbeds and noticed a few things out of place...

A FATEFUL FESTIVAL

Can you spot the six clues left in the herb garden?

PUZZLEBY GAZETTE

VILLAGE NEWSLETTER

PUZZLE 85

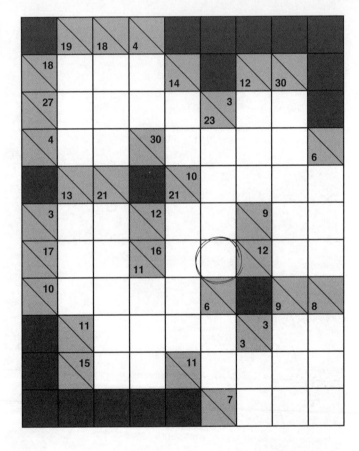

PUZZLEBY GAZETTE

VILLAGE NEWSLETTER

PUZZLE SECTION

PUZZLE 86

3 letters
Air
Auk
Chi
Don
Our
Rut

4 letters
Anti
Mien
Nova
Pods
Sift
Slew

6 letters
Desert
Trucks

7 letters
Cockpit
Melodic
Scherzo
Tigress

8 letters
Admonish
Intimate
Outsmart
Pendulum
Selfless
Sloshing

9 letters
Calibrate
Cellulite
Extension
Propagate

10 letters
Commission
Matchboxes
Predictive
Underskirt

A FATEFUL FESTIVAL

BURIED IN THE MUD was a frilly, red ribbon. I picked it up to admire it in more detail and try to discern any identifying feature. The ribbon was quite small, due to the parish council's declaration that large pins were too ostentatious. What was more, the ribbon's owner had apparently taken issue with their placement; the stitching was half-unpicked, making it hard to read the prize. Nevertheless, my keen eyes could still make it out…

Using the remaining letters, figure out what the ribbon says.

PUZZLE
87

WO_D_N   S_O_N   _ _NN_ _
B_S_   SH_ _ _B_ _ _D   _ _MP_T_ _I_N

A FATEFUL FESTIVAL

WITH NOT ONE, but two new clues under my belt, I knew I had
to hurry back to the village hall to check the records and find the
competitors from past baking competitions.

Baskerville began to sniff his way back out of the garden, but thankfully,
Cat and I wouldn't have to follow his winding path back to the middle of the
village; there was a bridge over the river that would take me straight there.

"Come, Baskerville—this way!" I called. "We must hurry!"

*Solve the bridge puzzle to help Miss Hemmingway get back to
the village hall.*

PUZZLE 88

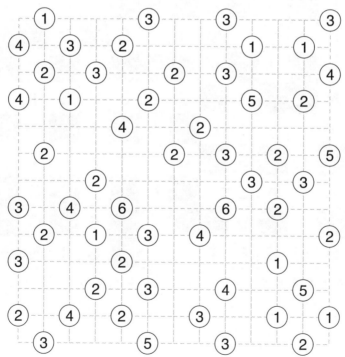

PUZZLEBY GAZETTE
VILLAGE NEWSLETTER

PUZZLE
89

E	X	I	L	E				T	T	E	R	Y
				X		O				E		
		E		T		K		F	I	L		S
E	M	B	A	R	K	E	D		P		I	
L		A		E		R		A	O	R	T	A
L	A	N		M	A		S		D			
E		A		E						L		T
N		T		E	F	F	U	S	I			E
T		I	D		A		I					R
	L		S		G		Z	Z	L	I		
A		A	S			L				S		L
			U			◯		E		O		O
S	W	E	E	T				S	I	N	E	

A B C D E F G H I J K L M N O P Q R S T U V W X Y Z

PUZZLE 90

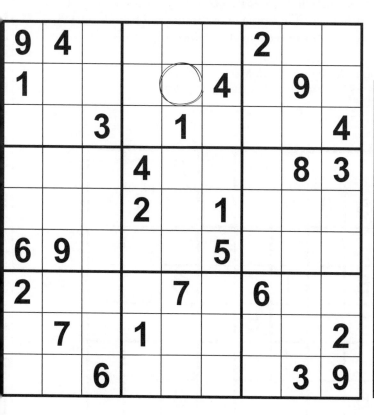

A FATEFUL FESTIVAL

CREEPING INTO THE ARCHIVE ROOM, I set about trying to find the document I needed. The room was full of filing cabinets, all properly polished, such was the tireless dedication of the caretaker, Miss May Isaac. Personally, I thought some of the gala's fundraising should go towards some extra shelving; some of the files were spilling onto the floor.

Cat bounded up the open drawers as though they were a staircase, before pausing curiously. He pawed at one drawer in disgust and hissed. When I went to see why, I realized the drawer smelled faintly of lemons.

PUZZLE 91

Solve the jigsaw sudoku to build the chests of drawers for Cat to jump up.

						2	4	
	5	9	3				6	2
		◯			1			
	8		1			6		
	1			5				
			4					
5	6					3		
	3							
1					2			

A FATEFUL FESTIVAL

THE BAKING COMPETITION FOLDER within was heavy with years and competition stage numbers. After much searching through the drawer, I found the file I needed: records for last year's Shortbread Competition. I read through the ranked competitors and noted their addresses listed beside them—but the names were in Morse code, perhaps to avoid prying eyes spoiling the results.

Fortunately, I had a military friend who had taught me the code and, taking a pencil from my handbag, I quickly unscrambled the names.

*Use the code to figure out the
names of the competitors.*

1. -.-. .- -- .. -.-. .-.. .- .-   .... .- --. ..- .

2. -.. .- .... .-. .- .- .- .... .-   -.. .- .- .-.. .-.. .. .- -. .-. .

3. --. .-. .-- -- .-.   --. .-. .-. .... .--

4. .-.. ..- -.-. .-. ... .-.. .-. .-.. .-   .-.. .. ..- -.-. .-- -.-

5. .-- .. .- -. .-   .... .. -.-. .- .-. ..- --- .-. -..

PUZZLEBY GAZETTE
VILLAGE NEWSLETTER

YOUR HOROSCOPE FROM ACHILLIA HEADLAND

This is a week to have your cake and eat it too. The Libra moon calls for balance, so indulge in a biscuit or two while keeping an eye on your water intake. You deserve to be in full health, and to treat yourself too! However, beware emotionally raw Pluto, which might spur some people to act irrationally as it clashes with Libra.

3		6						1
	2				1			
		9		6	7			4
	4	8						2
5						9	8	
9			8	1		3		
			5				9	
1						7		8

PUZZLE 94

54			61	63					
	56			64	66			76	
		58	23		◯	70			78
50				19	15		71	80	81
48						1		83	
46				7		2			85
	44	30	27			5	11	87	
43		31						93	
40	41	37			100			92	
			34	98	97		91		

A FATEFUL FESTIVAL

AT LEAST FOUR OF THE ACCOMPANYING ADDRESSES, I realized, led to potential suspects, all of them bakers who might be holding a grudge against Paula Elstree for her snub. But which address housed the killer?

I squinted down at the page and held it further back as though that would make me see things from a new perspective. A scrawled message in the corner of the page caught my eye - a clue as to which address was right. Unfortunately, it wasn't to be an easy win; it was in the form of another riddle. Raising my torchlight, I put pencil to paper once more to figure out the house number of the most likely suspect.

PUZZLE
95

Solve the riddle to find out the house number.

1. The last digit is twice the first digit.

2. The sum of the first digit and the last digit is equal to the second digit.

3. The sum of all three digits is twice that of the second digit.

A FATEFUL FESTIVAL

I HURRIED BACK THROUGH THE QUIET STREETS with Cat, Baskerville huffing along alongside. An officer's peaked hat came into view as I made my way down Mulberry Lane, and I flagged down our amiable village policeman.

"Have you found something, Miss Hemmingway?" called D.C. Copper, striding over the cobbled street to meet me. He took his notepad out in preparation.

"I think so," I told him. "If my suspicions are correct, the culprit lives just down here..."

PUZZLE 96

Find the way through the maze to the address.

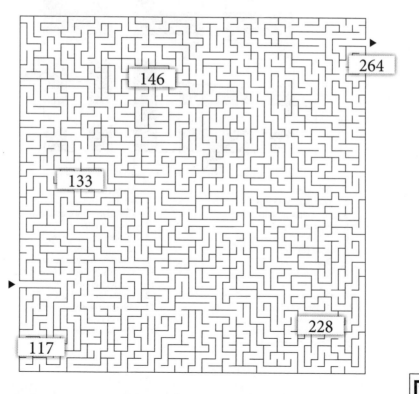

PUZZLE SECTION

PUZZLE
97

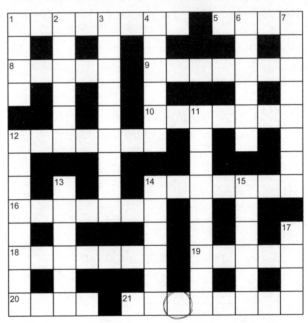

Across

1 Teachers (anag) (8)
5 Fit of shivering (4)
8 Flaring stars (5)
9 Shaving of the crown of head (7)
10 Dishonourable (7)
12 Terrible (7)
14 Frenzied (7)
16 Oppose an argument (7)
18 Beating (7)
19 Welcome (5)
20 The Christmas festival (4)
21 Cosmetic product for the skin (8)

Down

1 Female chickens (4)
2 Hollow in a solid object (6)
3 Alteration (9)
4 Impose or require (6)
6 Dirty; grimy (6)
7 Relating to critical explanation (8
11 Country in Central America (9)
12 In a friendly manner (8)
13 Edible bivalve mollusc (6)
14 Avoiding waste; thrifty (6)
15 Big cats (6)
17 Mix; agitate (4)

126

PUZZLEBY GAZETTE
VILLAGE NEWSLETTER

PUZZLE
98

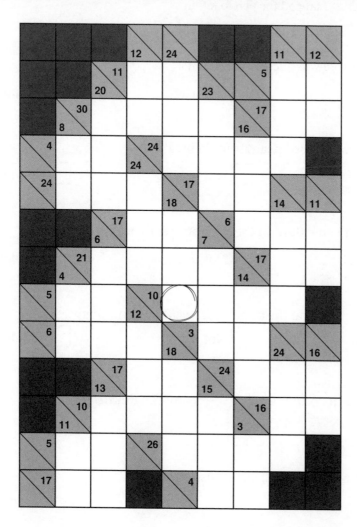

A FATEFUL FESTIVAL

AFTER THE EXCITEMENT OF THE PAST DAY OR SO, I sat down in my cozy winged armchair with some tea and shortbread to finalize my observations for D.C. Copper. Cat purred from his seat over my shoulders as I tapped the pen to my lips.

KNOWNS AND UNKNOWNS

Paula Elstree was allergic to peanuts.

☐ True   ☐ Not true   ☐ Unknown

The killer had used peanuts in their cake.

☐ True   ☐ Not true   ☐ Unknown

The killer came third in the previous year's baking contest.

☐ True   ☐ Not true   ☐ Unknown

The killer lived on the same street as Miss Hemmingway.

☐ True   ☐ Not true   ☐ Unknown

Did you decode the message from *The Puzzleby Gazette*?

_ _ _ _ _ _   _ _   _ _ _   _ _ _

Write the name of your main suspect below:

A FATEFUL FESTIVAL

CONCLUSION REACHED, I signed off on my notes and delivered them to D.C. Copper, who was pursing his lips as he stood at the scene of the crime, cookie in hand.

"Miss Hemmingway!" he sighed in relief. "Do you have your notes? I just want to be clear on a few things before I charge the murderer. What exactly happened?"

Which of these conclusions does Miss Hemmingway give?

1. Tragically, it had been Paula Elstree's peanut allergy that had killed her. Camilla Hague had used cake decorations that had been made in the same kitchen as her famous peanut brittle, the slight trace being enough for the judge to succumb.

2. Unhappy with her critique in the previous year's competition, Jean Hickford had vowed never to bake lavender shortbread again. She replanted her herb garden with belladonna, which she used to poison Paula Elstree's cup of tea.

3. Unable to reach her glass of water in time, poor Paula had choked on her forkful of lavender cake while judging the competition. Lucille Luck's perfectly thick royal icing on the sponge had been too tempting for Paula to resist, and she bit off more than she could chew.

CASE FOUR:

GIVING

UP THE

GHOST

INTRODUCTION

IT WAS A BEAUTIFUL, CRISP EARLY-AUTUMN MORNING IN PUZZLEBY, and Baskerville and I had been taking our morning stroll through the village. I decided to swing by the shops to pick up some flowers for myself, some pork chops for Baskerville and some salmon for Cat, who was sulking because I had washed his favorite blanket. I was just reaching for the perfect bunch of chrysanthemums from the florist's display when Deirdre Dalliance pulled up on her bicycle outside, squeaking to a halt and spooking my poor old Baskerville.

"The ghost of the Puzzleby Picker has struck again!" she announced breathlessly, hopping off the bike.

"No!" gasped Bessie Pygott, clutching her pearls and running out of the grocers. "Who is it this time?"

"Sam Haggle, the town planner," replied Deirdre, handing out this week's edition of *The Puzzleby Gazette*. "He was found up at the haunted mill."

Everyone murmured knowingly, and I rolled my eyes at Baskerville, who knew full well my thoughts on Puzzleby's resident phantom. In my experience, the only things that go bump in the night are old pipes.

Dahliah Dalliance, who had been sauntering past, showing off her new ostrich-feather hat around town, stopped to see what all the fuss was about.

"Haggle was a meddlesome fool," she declared, picking up a bunch of forget-me-nots and sniffing them dramatically. "He denied my request to erect a statue of myself in the village square and he couldn't even give me a good reason. Honestly, some people have no taste…"

Ghost or no ghost, there was a crime to investigate, and that meant my Saturday had just become decidedly more interesting.

"Come, Baskerville," I said, safely storing my chrysanthemums in my rolling cart and withdrawing my purse. "The game is on!"

GIVING UP THE GHOST

I HAVE ALWAYS LIVED MY LIFE by the principle that, when in doubt, one should turn to books. Thus, my first stop on this ghostly mystery was the Puzzleby library to find out a bit more about the local legend of the Puzzleby Picker. Upon arrival I saw that the library was closed, but the librarian, Ms Dickens, had left one of her famous riddles on the door. If I could solve it, I knew the answer would give me the code to open the library door.

Solve Ms Dickens' riddle to get into the library.

Popped to the shops (ran out of gin)
If you can solve this riddle, let yourself in!

My first is in spell, but not in book.
My second is in fright and also in shook.
My third is in cauldron, but never in pot.
My fourth is in net and also in knot.
My fifth is in bat, but never in vampire.
My sixth is in coal, but not found in fire.
My seventh is in moon, but not in night.

GIVING UP THE GHOST

VERY CLEVER, MS DICKENS, I thought with a wry smile. I had made it inside the library, but I knew the riddles wouldn't stop there. Since Ms Dickens utterly rejected the Dewey Decimal System (which she dubbed the 'Hooey' Decimal System), she had concocted her own book organization method called 'the Dickens Decimal System', the rules of which were entirely arbitrary and known only to her. Her code was lying out on the desk and I used it to find my quarry in the shelves.

PUZZLE
100

Solve the jigsaw sudoku to find the code for the book Miss Hemmingway is searching for in the grey boxes.

_ _ _ *Unpicking the Puzzleby Picker* by Nellie Yore.

	2			1	6		7	
3		7				8		
8	1							
	9		6					1
						2		
1		5						
		9						
					2			

GIVING UP THE GHOST

BOOK IN HAND, I skimmed the chapters to learn more about the Puzzleby Picker. According to the author, he was a young man who had come to Puzzleby in the 1800s to pick strawberries for the summer. He fell in love with a local woman but was murdered by her jealous husband, and his ghost had since been implicated in a number of suspected revenge killings of local men around the old mill over the years. All the victims had been killed in the same way and had been found with the same objects left on the body. However, when I reached the page describing the Puzzleby Picker's weapon of choice, I found the print obscured by a large tea stain, and I had to peer through the soggy mess to distinguish the letters.

PUZZLE 101

Complete the word search below to help Miss Hemmingway pinpoint the murder weapon. Which word is missing?

O	T	B	A	L	E	R	O	T	O	V	A	T	O	R
Y	W	H	E	E	L	P	L	O	U	G	H	P	R	I
F	R	O	N	T	E	N	D	L	O	A	D	E	R	L
E	E	G	I	R	C	U	L	T	I	V	A	T	O	R
T	I	E	H	R	O	C	D	R	S	P	L	K	W	O
K	F	K	C	U	R	T	T	F	I	L	K	R	O	F
C	I	A	A	V	K	I	A	N	L	J	O	O	R	Z
O	R	R	M	K	Z	O	G	R	P	E	W	F	R	P
T	A	Y	G	E	P	H	H	A	Y	J	X	Y	A	O
T	C	A	N	T	O	U	W	W	T	H	F	A	H	I
A	S	H	I	O	O	T	T	B	Z	O	O	H	C	P
M	U	C	K	S	P	R	E	A	D	E	R	E	S	A
W	R	E	L	K	N	I	R	P	S	D	L	E	I	F
V	L	L	I	R	D	D	E	E	S	U	O	A	D	P
E	T	R	M	B	R	E	T	S	E	V	R	A	H	T

AXE	HARVESTER	PITCHFORK
BALER	HAYFORK	REAPING-HOOK
CULTIVATOR	HAYRAKE	ROTARY HOE
DISC HARROW	IRRIGATOR	ROTOVATOR
FIELD SPRINKLER	MATTOCK	SCARIFIER
FORK-LIFT TRUCK	MILKING MACHINE	SEED DRILL
FRONT END LOADER	MUCKSPREADER	WHEEL PLOUGH

GIVING UP THE GHOST

I SAY, WHAT A TERRIBLE WAY TO GO! I decided to take *Unpicking the Puzzleby Picker* with me, thinking it may well come in handy. I flipped to the front of the book to jot down my name alongside everyone else who had borrowed it (if Ms Dickens wasn't going to be here to do her job, I suppose I should do it for her) and was surprised to see that the book had been checked out as recently as last week. Ms Dickens' handwriting was chaotic at the best of times, but if I squinted my eyes, I might be able to make it out who had borrowed the book last…

PUZZLE
102

Use the substitution code to find out the name of the last person to check 'Unpicking the Puzzleby Picker' out of the library.

TVY GVCCYR

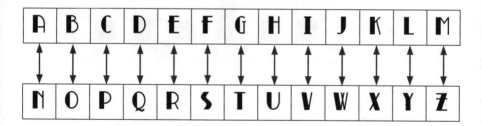

A	B	C	D	E	F	G	H	I	J	K	L	M
N	O	P	Q	R	S	T	U	V	W	X	Y	Z

PUZZLE 103

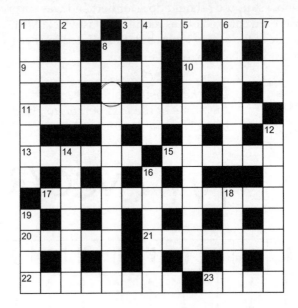

Across

1 Collide with (4)
3 Shields from (8)
9 Bodies of writing (7)
10 Form of expression (5)
11 Awe-inspiring (12)
13 Belonging to them (6)
15 Slender (6)
17 Evergreen shrub (12)
20 Major artery (5)
21 Serving no purpose (7)
22 Clip to keep something in place (8)
23 Large bodies of water (4)

Down

1 Say mean things about another (8)
2 ___ Simpson: cartoon character (5)
4 Cooks in the oven (6)
5 Insensitive to criticism (5-7)
6 Sophisticated hair style (7)
7 Japanese sport (4)
8 Person studying after a first degree (12)
12 Mesmerism (8)
14 Urges strongly (7)
16 Request earnestly (6)
18 Pass a rope through (5)
19 Young cow (4)

PUZZLEBY GAZETTE

VILLAGE NEWSLETTER

PUZZLE 104

7		9			5		6	
6	3							
				9				2
		7		4			1	
3		5		8				9
	8			7		4		
9		1						
							9	1
	6		7			3		4

Romancing the Miller's Wife by Dahliah Dalliance

Mr Oliver Dodd has long held a deep affection for Miss Aria Richards, and his heart was broken when she married the local miller, Mr Alexander Adams. When Mr Adams is found pinned to a windmill sail with a pitchfork, Oliver seizes his chance to woo his widow – but not everything is as it seems. Dahliah Dalliance's new thriller is bound to leave your head in a spin!

GIVING UP THE GHOST

WITH A DOG-EARED HISTORY BOOK UNDER MY ARM and a dog-eared Baskerville by my side, it was time to visit the crime scene. After a brief pitstop home to change into my Wellington boots and appease Cat with some salmon, Baskerville and I made our way across the fields to the old, abandoned mill. Unfortunately, the mill was on the other side of Farmer Frank's overgrown corn field. It was a good thing I'd come prepared for some cross-country walking!

PUZZLE
105

Help Miss Hemmingway and Baskerville get through the corn maze to the old mill.

GIVING UP THE GHOST

WE EMERGED FROM THE MAZE to find D.C. Copper standing just outside the old mill.

"Strange happenings, Miss Hemmingway," he said, nodding his head towards the mill. "The victim was found with a pitchfork sticking out of him and the whole place was locked up when we got here. No sign of a break-in, we had to cut off the padlock to get in there."

"How interesting," I mused. "I don't suppose you found an unusual assortment of items by the victim?"

D.C. Copper looked as though he had seen a ghost. "How did you know that?" he gasped. "Yes, there were flowers and fruit scattered all around the body." He produced a slip of paper. "The coroner's written it all in Latin and I haven't a clue. Perhaps you can make sense of it, Miss Hemmingway?" He shuddered. "I'm going for a cup of tea in the village, the whole thing is giving me the heebie-jeebies." With that, the detective departed, leaving me with another puzzle to solve. What a time to be alive!

PUZZLE 106

Solve the word scrambles to find out what type of fruit and flowers were found by the body.

LATIN NAME:	COMMON NAME:
Fragaria ananassa	BETRARSWYR
Myosotis arvensis	MONFET OG ERT

PUZZLE SECTION

PUZZLE 107

						4	6	5
	1		6	4	9			
	3							
6					8	1	3	
				7				
	4	8	2					9
							1	
			5	9	3		8	
2	6	3						

PUZZLE SECTION

PUZZLE
108

Across

8 100th anniversary (9)
9 Belonging to us (3)
10 Hankered after (5)
11 Wheeled supermarket vehicle (7)
12 ___ seat: aircraft safety device (7)
13 Unwrap a present (4)
17 Spheres (4)
18 Give up (7)
22 Spend lavishly (7)
24 Live by (5)
25 Pouch; enclosed space (3)
26 Medical practitioner (9)

Down

1 Go away from quickly (5)
2 At work (2-3-3)
3 Judgement (7)
4 Military drum signal (6)
5 Large mast (5)
6 Small body of water (4)
7 Making a petition to God (7)
14 Highly productive (8)
15 Have (7)
16 Not legally recognized; void (7)
19 Farewell remark (3-3)
20 Stage items (5)
21 Clothing made from denim (5)
23 Clay (anag) (4)

GIVING UP THE GHOST

IHAVE ALWAYS FOUND D.C. Copper's baricades to be a rather flimsy deterrent. I left Baskerville outside (he's far too old for such gruesome sights) and, ducking gracefully under the rope barrier, made my way into the old mill. Poor Mr Haggle had been—rather haphazardly, I noted—covered with a sheet, and my eye was caught by some blood-covered papers poking out from underneath. It looked like a development proposal for some land in Puzzleby. Could this be another clue to explain his murder?

PUZZLE 109

Use the A1 Z26 cipher (A=1) to decode the coordinates below, then plot them on the grid to find the piece of land that Sam Haggle was selling. The first letter of each pair refers to the bottom row and the second letter to the left-hand side.

(G,H) (D,F) (C,H) (F,F) (E,H) (F,E) (D,G)
(E,F) (F,H) (E,G) (H,F) (F,G) (G,F) (G,G)

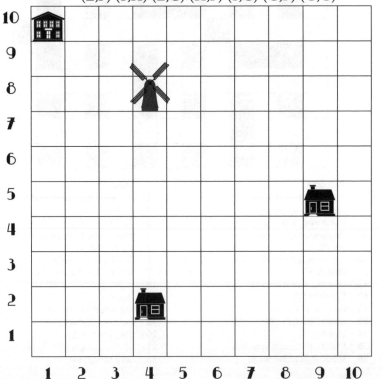

GIVING UP THE GHOST

A HAUNTED MILL INDEED! Someone certainly seemed upset about the possibility of it falling into a developer's hands. Underneath the map of Puzzleby was a handwritten note. Perhaps this would reveal what Mr Haggle was planning to do with the land? If it weren't for all these pesky bloodstains, I'm sure I'd be able to make it out…

Solve the arrow words then unscramble the circled letters to figure out what Sam Haggle was proposing to build on the land.

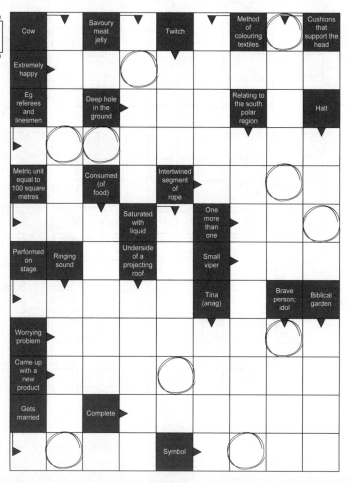

PUZZLE
110

PUZZLEBY GAZETTE
VILLAGE NEWSLETTER

PUZZLE 111

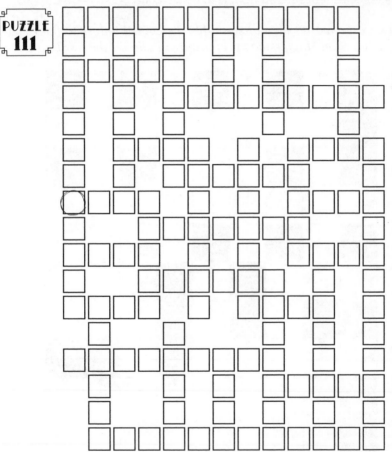

4 letters
Anon
Aura
Garb
Gods
Hire
Inns
Puma
Rump
Sari
Seer

5 letters
Adieu
Anger
Hopes
Inane
Noses
Stash

6 letters
Divest
Easter
Eclair
Outwit

7 letters
Bigness
Custard
Omnibus
Pebbles
Retsina

8 letters
Arpeggio
Irritant

9 letters
Standards
Tradesman

12 letters
Inadequately
Triumphantly
Unacceptable
Unhesitating

PUZZLE SECTION

PUZZLE
112

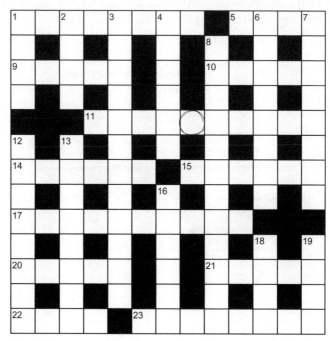

Across

1 Rocked (8)
5 Musical composition (4)
9 Put an idea in someone's mind (5)
10 Stanza of a poem (5)
11 Deliberate (10)
14 Immature of its kind (of insects) (6)
15 Male fertilizing flower organ (6)
17 Analogy (10)
20 Vigorous attack (5)
21 Coral reef (5)
22 Chickens lay these (4)
23 Speaking many languages (8)

Down

1 Jar lids (4)
2 Type of wood (4)
3 Lavish event (12)
4 Special ___ : film illusion (6)
6 Type of employment (4-4)
7 Traveling too quickly (8)
8 Developmental (12)
12 Easily calmed (8)
13 Making waves in hair (8)
16 Ludicrous failure (6)
18 Useful implement (4)
19 List (anag) (4)

GIVING UP THE GHOST

IT HAD CERTAINLY BEEN A FRUITFUL TRIP, no pun intended, of course. I was just about to make my way back into the village when I spotted something tiny and wriggling on an uncovered part of the body. Fortunately, I once rode the Trans-Siberian Railway with an Austrian forensic entomologist and learned a great deal about how blow flies can be used to determine time of death. I bent down—not too close, mind you—to inspect further.

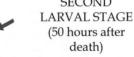

PUZZLE
113

Match the blow fly
Miss Hemmingway found on the body
to the life cycle stage below.

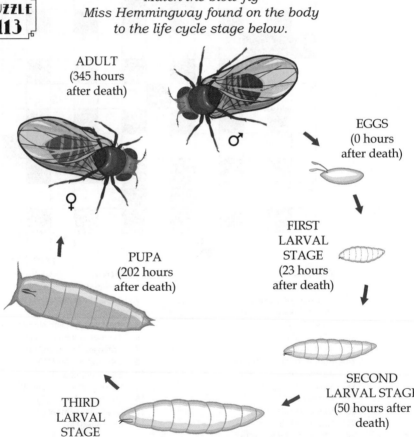

ADULT
(345 hours
after death)

♂

EGGS
(0 hours
after death)

FIRST
LARVAL
STAGE
(23 hours
after death)

PUPA
(202 hours
after death)

♀

SECOND
LARVAL STAGE
(50 hours after
death)

THIRD
LARVAL
STAGE
(72 after death)

GIVING UP THE GHOST

I KNEW FROM **D.C. COPPER** that the body had been found at 8:12am that morning, which was a Saturday. And now, right in my hand, I had a piece of wriggling evidence that could help us pin down the victim's time of death. Gosh, I do love science.

Using your answer from the previous page, which of these is the most likely window for the victim's time of death?

| THURSDAY | FRIDAY | SATURDAY |

PUZZLEBY GAZETTE

VILLAGE NEWSLETTER

PUZZLE 115

	I	M	I	S		S		S	O	S		S	
E		A			I	N	C		B	A	T	E	
	W	N		E		A		L					
G		T	R	A		L		I	C	E			
R		R		E						E			
E		A	C	T		S	O	C	I	E	T		
			O		T				N				
R	A	I	N		O	W			G	R	E		
	C		U			P				E			
	E	B	U			M	U	D	G	E			
	T		N		P		I					E	N
M	I	S	C		I	E	F			E			G
	C		T		N				O	D	L	E	

A B C D E F G H I J K L M N O P Q R S T U V W X Y Z

PUZZLEBY GAZETTE
VILLAGE NEWSLETTER

PUZZLE 116

1	25	23	4	11	18	23	17		23	25	23	23
3		21		10		22				4		3
8	11	4	3	10		2	11	24	7	23	10	18
20		23		6		1				14		4
		10		4		23	10	12	6	7	4	23
19	23	10	18	23	4	10		6		20		11
11				17				7				18
9		11		16		10	6	26	10	7	17	8
23	3	22	4	8	25	18		26		15		
16		6				4		16		25		26
7	15	15	23	4	10	23		7	15	11	21	23
3		23				13		3		22		9
10	11	3	5		5	3	7	21	2	18	16	8

A B C D E F G H I J K L M N O P Q R S T U V W X Y Z

1	2	3	4	5	6	7	8	9	10	11	12	13
			R									

14	15	16	17	18	19	20	21	22	23	24	25	26
			D								P	

149

GIVING UP THE GHOST

WITH MY WORK AT THE CRIME SCENE ALL WRAPPED UP, I made my way back outside to find Baskerville snoozing in the early afternoon sun.

"Come now, lazy bones," I told him. "Time to get to work. We are certainly not going back the way we came, there must be a simpler route back to the village, or at least one that won't have me picking twigs out of my hair for days to come." Baskerville immediately set about sniffing at the ground, like the well-trained sleuthing sidekick that he was. "That's the spirit, Baskerville!"

PUZZLE
117

Complete the king's journey puzzle to help Baskerville find a shortcut back to the village.

			5						61
9			15		1			63	
	13	18			37	57	65		
					44				69
20		34			45			73	71
21		40		46					
	30			53	81	91			76
23						93	94	95	
			51					98	100
25					85		88		

GIVING UP THE GHOST

SAFELY BACK IN THE VILLAGE—in record time thanks to a surprisingly sprightly Baskerville—my first stop was Pygott's Grocery Store. I asked Bessie if she remembered anyone (human or phantom) purchasing any forget-me-nots recently.

"I don't need to remember, Miss Hemmingway," Bessie replied brightly. "I always write down every sale, otherwise I forget to restock!"

What a stroke of luck! Bessie noted that she had indeed sold three bunches of forget-me-nots on Wednesday morning, but unfortunately she had dripped candle wax all over the customer's name.

PUZZLE 118

Solve the kriss kross puzzle then unscramble the letters in the circles to find out who bought forget-me-nots from Bessie.

3 letters
Ate
Chi
Eke
Nap
Pep
Too
Yew

4 letters
Apes
Earn
Eyed
Kerb
Navy
Pant
Pods
Rear
Slot
Woke

5 letters
Buffs
Sieve

6 letters
Eyries
Sashay

7 letters
Capsize
Creased
Kinship
Novelty
Omitted
Origami
Pinhole
Ravioli

8 letters
Backbite
Engineer
Mechanic
Sportive

9 letters
Aspartame
Fieldwork

PUZZLE SECTION

PUZZLE 119

PUZZLE 120

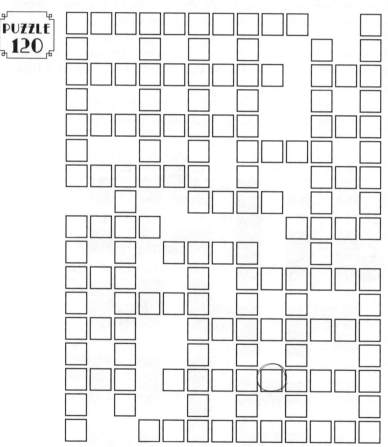

3 letters
Ant
Lea
Nag
Oat
Our
Owl

4 letters
Fawn
Hero
Hide
Kilo
Liar
Shed

6 letters
Exults
Fronds

7 letters
Ovation
Scenery
Stoical
Tranche

8 letters
Airbrush
Concerto
Economic
Nuisance
Officers
Supposed

9 letters
Autograph
Footloose
Immediate
Litigator

10 letters
Accusingly
Foundation
Trespasser
Unworkable

GIVING UP THE GHOST

IT WAS CERTAINLY SPOOKY how many times that name had come up in my investigations so far, so I decided to drop into the village tearoom, The Gil Tea Party, for a spot of afternoon tea with a side of sleuthing. I ordered a pot of Earl Grey and a scone, and invited Gil to sit with me. At the risk of becoming the specter at the feast, I asked Gil how he felt about Sam Haggle's plans to build a coffee shop in the village.

"No skin off my nose, Miss Hemmingway," replied Gil cheerily. "I'm shutting up shop and moving to the coast next month anyway." He showed me a pamphlet advertising an idyllic-looking seaside town, although his tea-stained fingers were covering up the town's name…

PUZZLE 121

Solve the A-Z puzzle then unscramble the letters in the circles to find the name of the seaside town Gil is moving to.

_O_ _ _ _ _ _   _ _ _E

WHEN GIL STOOD UP TO FETCH MORE TEA, a train
ticket fell out from between the pages of the pamphlet. Not meaning
to pry, but absolutely needing to investigate, I took a quick glance at the
information on the ticket. I was particularly interested in the time and date of
Gil's journey.

PUZZLE
122

742123

DEP: THURSDAY _ . _ _PM

RETURN: FRIDAY _ . _ _PM

742123

*Solve the
sudoku to fill
in the missing
information
on Gil's train
ticket.*

		4		7				1
			9	6	4	5		
			5			6	2	
	4					1		7
2		9					3	
	6	8			5			
		7	8	1	2			
1				4		7		

PUZZLEBY GAZETTE

VILLAGE NEWSLETTER

PUZZLE 123

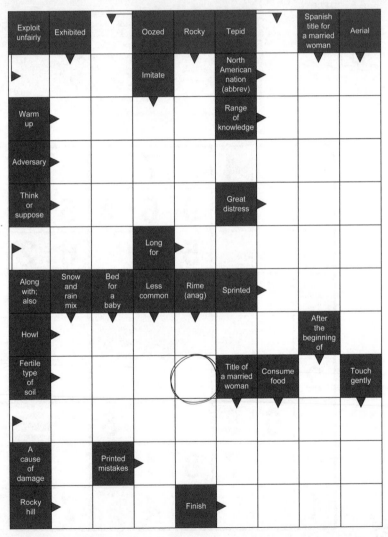

A crossword-style grid puzzle with the following clues:

Exploit unfairly	Exhibited			Oozed	Rocky	Tepid	Spanish title for a married woman	Aerial
				Imitate		North American nation (abbrev)		
Warm up					Range of knowledge			
Adversary								
Think or suppose					Great distress			
				Long for				
Along with; also	Snow and rain mix	Bed for a baby	Less common	Rime (anag)	Sprinted			
Howl							After the beginning of	
Fertile type of soil					Title of a married woman	Consume food		Touch gently
A cause of damage		Printed mistakes						
Rocky hill					Finish			

PUZZLEBY GAZETTE

VILLAGE NEWSLETTER

PUZZLE 124

9								
		5	7		3			
	8			9	5	2	6	
	4		1			3		
			3	7	6			
		6			2		1	
	6	1	2	5			3	
			6		4	1		
								8

GIVING UP THE GHOST

PERHAPS **I** WAS LOOKING FOR MOTIVE in the wrong place. But I still had questions for our resident tea party planner.

"Do you have a particular interest in the Puzzleby Picker, Gil?" I asked.

"Hmm, not until recently," he admitted. "I had a booking for a Puzzleby Picker themed tea party for the Puzzleby Historical Society on Wednesday. I was surprised it went ahead," he added thoughtfully. "Since I couldn't fulfil half of the menu items they requested on account of my strawberry allergy."

"Is that so?" I asked, with interest.

"'Fraid so," nodded Gil. "Can't even be in the same room as them."

PUZZLE 125

Unscramble the menu items to find out if Gil is telling the truth about not serving strawberries.

MENU

BAWECHUMS DUNCCIERS

CARRIAT POTTS

FUMBLUENY BIRFERS

YAPERCAST SHROBKERR

BAMCKLEBRY RAJ

GIVING UP THE GHOST

"So that's why you bought forget-me-nots!"** I pressed. Gil looked momentarily taken aback, then laughed.

"Nothing gets past you does it, Miss Hemmingway? That's right, I borrowed a book about the Puzzleby Picker from the library to make sure I got all the details right. I take my tea parties very seriously," he finished proudly. "The lady who made the booking was so impressed that she took all the flowers home with her."

My ears certainly picked up at that. I asked Gil for the name of the person who made the booking.

"I tell you what," he began, scribbling something down. "I know how much you love puzzles, so why don't I let you work it out yourself? Think of this as your personal, puzzle-themed tea party."

PUZZLE 126

Use the code to find out who booked the Puzzleby Picker tea party.

a	b	c	d	e	f	g	h	i	j
⌐	⊔	L	⊐	□	⊏	⌐	⊓	Γ	⌐•

k	l	m	n	o	p	q	r	s	t
⌐•	L•	⊐•	⊐•	⊏•	⌐•	⌐•	Γ•	V	>

u	v	w	x	y	z				
<	∧	⌄	·>	<·	∧				

PUZZLE SECTION

Across

1 Where darts players throw from (4)
3 Formal agreement (8)
9 Concealed (7)
10 Unable to function properly (of a leg) (5)
11 Best starting placement in a motor race (4,8)
14 Former measure of length (3)
16 Recycle (5)
17 Sense of self-esteem (3)
18 Dimly; not clearly (12)
21 Harsh and serious in manner (5)
22 Italian rice dish (7)
23 Branch of metaphysics (8)
24 Military force (4)

Down

1 Busy and active (8)
2 Small crude shelter (5)
4 Not new (3)
5 Fellowship (12)
6 One of two gaps in a shirt (7)
7 Playthings (4)
8 Commensurate (12)
12 Gush out in a jet (5)
13 Plump (4-4)
15 Opposite of shortest (7)
19 Teacher (5)
20 Capital of Norway (4)
22 Piece of cloth (3)

PUZZLEBY GAZETTE
VILLAGE NEWSLETTER

PUZZLE 128

	21	23	6	6	23	18	11	16	1	23	4	
16		14		24		23		24		1		13
19		21		4	23	19	23	14		5	21	21
23	1	3	6	4		16		10		10		5
18		4		21		7		23	14	6	18	9
23	1	6	18	23	15	23	4					25
1		4		4				5		10		18
13					20	18	5	26	26	3	6	3
16	14	4	23	6		23		26		6		20
4		12		5		17		3	18	3	4	2
23	15	24		4	14	23	23	18		8		6
22		3		6		10		15		23		4
	5	22	19	23	18	6	3	4	3	14	20	

A B C D E F G H I J K L M N O P Q R S T U V W X Y Z

1	2	3	4	5	6	7	8	9	10	11	12	13
											Q	

14	15	16	17	18	19	20	21	22	23	24	25	26
						G						F

161

GIVING UP THE GHOST

BASKERVILLE AND **I** DEPARTED The Gil Tea Party and made our way across the square to the offices of Nellie Yore, Chairwoman of the Puzzleby Historical Society. The news of the Puzzleby Picker's attack had obviously spread like wildfire, and there were more people in the street with souvenirs than I had ever seen before. But that wasn't the only noticeable difference that I spotted at the Puzzleby Historical Society that day.

GIVING UP THE GHOST

*Spot the five differences
between the two scenes.*

PUZZLE 130

					1				
6				20	23	35			39
8							45		
9	14					48		50	42
		26	32				54	53	
16			58			99		79	
				92	100	97	96		
		68	89				85	82	
	64		69		87		84		
62									75

PUZZLE SECTION

PUZZLE 131

Grid (rows top to bottom; blank = shaded cell):

	20		20		1		20		17		11	
2	17	17	22	7	21	1	5	26	14	7	6	23
	23		21		2		9		17		17	
14	1	10	26	20	16	7	15		26	2	17	10
			12		18		23		15		15	
1	19	23	20	8	1	6		22	20	1	6	8
	21				23		16				26	
14	7	21	19	20		4	9	1	6	26	5	23
	1		7		3		21		23			
20	24	7	18		26	10	5	7	10	15	7	15
	17		1		22		11		25		1	
13	9	21	26	20	22	21	9	15	7	10	2	7
	5		6		23		6			20		16

A B C D E F G H I J K L M N O P Q R S T U V W X Y Z

1	2	3	4	5	6	7	8	9	10	11	12	13
						O					F	G

14	15	16	17	18	19	20	21	22	23	24	25	26
			O									

165

GIVING UP THE GHOST

WHEN **I** FINALLY PUSHED THROUGH THE CROWDS and made my way inside, Nellie Yore was too preoccupied taking bookings for next week's Puzzleby Picker Ghost Tour to even notice me. While her back was turned, I took the opportunity to sneak a peek at her bookings over the past few days. I could see that there was something written under Friday's entry, but the message had been scribbled over with thick pen. However, when I turned the page over, I could see the markings of the original message on the underside, but it was back-to-front. I'd have to decode it quickly before Nellie turned around…

PUZZLE
132

Decode the back-to-front message to find out what was written in Friday's entry in Nellie's appointment book.

GIVING UP THE GHOST

THE PIECES WERE STARTING TO FALL INTO PLACE. I wondered where my investigation might take me next. I decided to take the weight off and partake in a spot of puzzling in the newsletter to allow my wheels to keep turning in the background. However, it seemed as though the 10th word I reached in the newsletter's pathfinder puzzle was pointing my wheels in a very specific direction.

PUZZLE
133

Can you figure out where Miss Hemmingway should go next?

P	L	U	S	R	E	P	P	O	C
H	B	U	B	U	E	R	D	E	R
A	N	N	R	N	S	L	O	H	P
T	O	S	E	C	E	T	I	M	P
E	I	T	L	Y	L	B	R	A	L
G	O	U	I	N	C	I	R	E	C
G	G	L	E	D	U	R	I	C	N
L	S	O	R	T	D	C	N	L	A
E	L	E	N	E	O	R	G	A	B
S	F	U	N	S	T	T	U	B	E

Balance, Bunsen Burner, Clamp Holder, Copper Sulphate, Crucible, Cylinder, Funnel, Goggles, Solution, Stirring Rod, Test Tube

PUZZLEBY GAZETTE
VILLAGE NEWSLETTER

PUZZLE 134

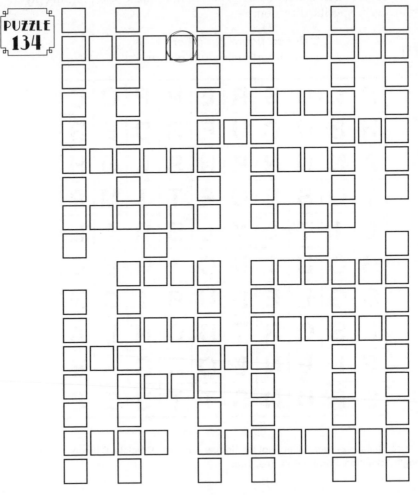

3 letters
Boa
Coy
Ell
Ski
Ton
Tub

4 letters
Bran
Club
Ebbs
Else
Pier
Pint
Posh
Rued

6 letters
Anoint
Earths
Tiling
Tutors

7 letters
Anodyne
Nibbled

8 letters
Assesses
Bagpiper
Confetti
Elevator
Escapist
Initiate
Malaysia
Subtract
Thanking
Wretched

9 letters
Egotistic
Embattled

PUZZLEBY GAZETTE
VILLAGE NEWSLETTER

PUZZLE
135

YOUR HOROSCOPE FROM ACHILLIA HEADLAND

The Mars retrograde is still with us. It is truly rare for it to last this long, and now it's coming into Aries, the warrior planet's home. This conjunction often inspires us to focus on change—but beware; it can also inspire recklessness, violence, and even war. This week will necessitate careful planning to make the most of the feelings it may bring.

A fact that has been verified	▼	A dancer or singer	Handouts (anag)		Donation	▼		Local inhabitant	Saw; observed
					Single in number			▼	▼
Rapid spin of the body		Test again (2-7)	Nocturnal bird of prey		Negative vote				
▶		▼	▼						
					Relieve or free from				
Stitches	▶								
Large Israeli city (3,4)	▶								Go out of a place
▶			Serbian monetary unit		Insect that can sting				▼
Magic spell	Increase in amount	▶			Settee		Decorated a cake	
▶			Agitate a liquid	▼				
——— Moore: Hollywood actress	Type of bill	▶		▶				
▶			Enemies	▶				
Fish	Short trips on another's behalf							

169

GIVING UP THE GHOST

OF COURSE I SHOULD VISIT THE POLICE STATION! No doubt D.C Copper would be in need of my assistance.

He was deep in thought when I entered the station with Baskerville, and the poor man dropped his papers all over the floor in fright. Once he had collected himself, he told me that a second blood profile had been left behind at the crime scene. When I pointed out that ghosts didn't bleed, D.C. Copper looked rather sheepish, but I spared his blushes by busying myself with the details on the coroner's report. However, the coroner's handwriting looked more like a spider had gone tap dancing across the paper, and I had to employ my sharpest decoding skills to read the results.

Complete the crossword puzzle on the next page and use the letters in the circles to find the missing final pair of chromosomes.

Profile: Sam Haggle

TEST	VALUE
Haemoglobin	8.0
Protein	279
Red cell count	3.86
White cell count	27.1
Thrombocytes	462
Glucose	12.9
Sodium	127
Potassium	4.2
Creatinine	40
Gender profile	XY

Profile: Unknown

TEST	VALUE
Haemoglobin	8.2
Protein	280
Red cell count	3.70
White cell count	27
Thrombocytes	460
Glucose	13
Sodium	130
Potassium	4.4
Creatinine	45
Gender profile	_ _

GIVING UP THE GHOST

PUZZLE
136

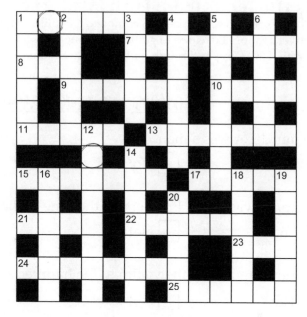

Across
1 Urge (6)
7 Fee paid to use someone's services when required (8)
8 Tack (3)
9 Ball-shaped object (6)
10 Mite (anag) (4)
11 Thin roofing slabs (5)
13 Attack (7)
15 Stinging plants (7)
17 The furnishings in a room (5)
21 Engage in argument (4)
22 Respiratory condition (6)
23 Eg pecan or cashew (3)
24 Vehicle (8)
25 Eg Sir and Dame (6)

Down
1 Liveliness (6)
2 ___ and Gretel: fairy tale (6)
3 Put in considerable effort (5)
4 Non-believer in God (7)
5 Take legal action (8)
6 Breakfast food (6)
12 Coming from outside (8)
14 Corrupt (7)
16 Give a job to (6)
18 French fashion designer (6)
19 Paths (6)
20 Begin (5)

GIVING UP THE GHOST

WITH THE BLOOD PROFILES OF THE VICTIM and the mysterious second person complete, I felt like I was nearing the end of my investigation. I decided to gather all my notes together, put the kettle on and walk D.C. Copper through what I had discovered.

KNOWNS AND UNKNOWNS

The murderer was a man.

☐ True ☐ Not true ☐ Unknown

Gil Tipple was not in Puzzleby at the time of the murder.

☐ True ☐ Not true ☐ Unknown

The murderer drove the victim to the haunted mill.

☐ True ☐ Not true ☐ Unknown

Before the murder, the Puzzleby Historical Society was going out of business.

☐ True ☐ Not true ☐ Unknown

Did you decode the message from *The Puzzleby Gazette*?

___ _____ ____ ____

Write the name of your main suspect below:

GIVING UP THE GHOST

CONCLUSION REACHED, I pushed myself up from the station's kitchen table and brought my findings to D.C. Copper.

Rapping sharply on his office door, I stepped inside and set a cup of tea down on his desk. "Drink that quickly, Detective," I told him. "You've got a murderer to arrest!"

Which of these conclusions does Miss Hemmingway give?

1. Knowing that the demolition of the haunted mill would be the final nail in the coffin for the Puzzleby Historical Society, Chairwoman Nellie Yore lured Sam Haggle to the haunted mill with the offer of a free tour. Once there, she murdered him with a pitchfork, cutting her hand in the struggle and leaving her DNA at the scene. Being the world's preeminent Puzzleby Picker expert, Nellie was able to convincingly stage the crime scene to look like the Puzzleby Picker had struck again.

2. Distraught at the prospect of having to compete with a fancy new coffee shop, Gil Tipple decided to take matters into his own hands. He borrowed a book from the library to research the Puzzleby Picker and waited for Sam Haggle to turn up at the haunted mill. Then, he murdered him with a pitchfork and placed forget-me-nots and strawberries around the body to make it look like an attack by the Puzzleby Picker.

3. Furious that his favorite haunt was to be destroyed in favour of a coffee shop, the ghost of the Puzzleby Picker did indeed rise once more to slay the man responsible for the development. He drifted through the locked door of the haunted mill and murdered Sam Haggle using his trademark murder weapon in a bitter act of vengeance and spite.

CASE FIVE:

THE CURIOUS

CASE OF THE

CAT IN THE

NIGHTTIME

INTRODUCTION

SHOCKWAVES RANG THROUGHOUT PUZZLEBY, and not merely because of the ferocious thunderstorm. Father Featherby, our beloved local priest, had been found dead in the St Cryptus crypt.

"You know," said Dahliah, who had come over to drop off cherry cake to celebrate my birthday, along with Deirdre, who brought my copy of *The Puzzleby Gazette*. "Just the other day, I saw Deacon Beacon having an argument with our dear Priest. It wasn't just me who saw, it was half the congregation. Something about missing funds for the church roof..."

"Not every argument ends in a murder, Mom. By that logic, YOU could be the murderer, after you had that fight with Father Featherby a few weeks back."

Dahliah pursed her lips as if she'd smelled something unpleasant. "Don't start with me, Deirdre, dear." She turned to me and explained: "It was only a little disagreement. You see, I have a new book coming out. It's just a little racy, you know. And I thought, the main character being a priest and all, it would be rather fun to do a reading at the chapel — after dark, candles, all very tasteful. But dear Father Featherby wasn't willing to compromise. All water under the bridge, now, as they say."

THE CURIOUS CASE OF THE CAT IN THE NIGHTTIME

DAHLIAH AND FATHER FEATHERBY'S disagreement may be water under the bridge, but the recent thunderstorm had left rather a lot of water on top of the bridge, so I had to find an alternate route to the chapel. I was about to give up and lift my skirts to start paddling, when I noticed that a local strongman had heaved some big slabs of paving into some semblance of a line across the flood. Fortunately, I have always been somewhat spry, so I was able to hop quickly over the makeshift stepping-stones easily.

Solve the bridge puzzle below to help Miss Hemmingway across the flood.

PUZZLE
137

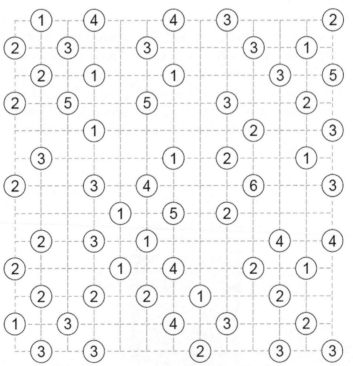

THE CHAPEL WAS SHROUDED IN SHADOWS; a testament, perhaps, to the sadness that hung over our little village. Even the yew trees on either side of the entrance looked sad and droopy, showing little of that deep, forest green for which they were known. Father Featherby's keys were hanging by the heavy wooden door, but if I tried each of them, I would be there all day. Luckily, there was a hint on a post-it next to the lock. Hmm... I would need to dust off my algebra skills for this one!

Solve the puzzle to work out which key opens the chapel door.

$$\begin{array}{r} \text{GET} \\ + \text{THE} \\ \hline \text{KEY} \end{array}$$

PUZZLE
138

137

425

281

004

916

821

13

25

PUZZLEBY GAZETTE
VILLAGE NEWSLETTER

PUZZLE
139

S	S		J					C		P
	S	O	B	A	R		C	O	R	N
					P		N			
F	R	E	E	Z	E	R		S	I	N	C	E
O	H						O		Y	
L	O	O			I	D	O	L		
D			R		A		E		C		H
		M	E	E	T	S		P	U		A
O				O		W		B			
	I		O		R	A	I	N	I	N	G
O		O		I		Y			C		
E	R	R	A		A		O	C	T	A	V	E
S		D		E					L		D

A B C D E F G H I J K L M N O P Q R S T U V W X Y Z

Fortune and Fate by Dahliah Dalliance

A trip to the local circus soon goes wrong when Mr. and Mrs. Joshua Johnson are found dead behind the mystic's tent. Fortune Teller Claire Voyant is immediately arrested for their murder, but Miss Abigail Tansley suspects foul play. She is joined in her investigation by Detective Frank Silver, but the pair might be heading into more danger than they realise in this towering triumph of a thriller from Dahliah Dalliance.

PUZZLEBY GAZETTE
VILLAGE NEWSLETTER

PUZZLE
140

2			10			22		24	
1							29	28	
7	14		33					64	
15	17			92			70	65	60
			100	98			78		
			97			84		72	
37		47	96	89			76		
				87	86			56	
	40		43		50				54

179

ONCE **I H**AD **SELECTED THE RIGHT KEY**, the lock clicked open easily. Stepping carefully over the heavy stone doorstep, I flicked on the switch and the lights hummed into life, illuminating the musty interior of the church. It looked a bit worse for wear, and as I peered around, I saw that the building had deteriorated since the last time I had been there.

THE CURIOUS CASE OF THE CAT IN THE NIGHTTIME

Spot the five differences between the two scenes.

PUZZLEBY GAZETTE

VILLAGE NEWSLETTER

PUZZLE 142

8							2	
7					3		4	
	5		8	9		1	6	
				3	9	6		
				6				
		5	7	8				
	2	1		5	8		3	
	8		6					2
	7							1

PUZZLE
143

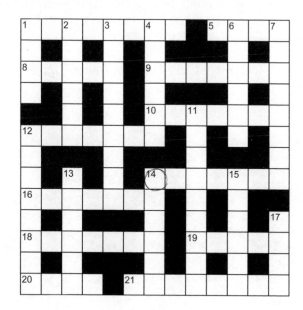

Across

1 Doorway (8)
5 Jelly or culture medium (4)
8 Basic units of an element (5)
9 Envelops (7)
10 Alphabetical lists (7)
12 Designer of trendy clothes (7)
14 Feeling guilty (7)
16 Beg (7)
18 Garden flower (7)
19 ___ Nash: writer of light verse (5)
20 Helps (4)
21 Cosiness (8)

Down

1 Vivacity (4)
2 Causing distress or trouble (6)
3 Link (9)
4 Approval; recognition (6)
6 Massive system of stars (6)
7 Held out against (8)
11 Compound vowel character (9)
12 Flowering plant (5,3)
13 Specified (6)
14 Reach (6)
15 Confuse (6)
17 Ceases (4)

THE CURIOUS CASE OF THE CAT IN THE NIGHTTIME

I WENT INTO THE BACK ROOM AND LOOKED AROUND. The argument between Deacon Beacon and Father Featherby had, according to Dahliah, been over some missing funds for the roof repairs, which I could see now were sorely needed — I had sidled around several puddles on my way through the church. Father Featherby, something of a traditionalist, kept all his records by hand in large leather tomes, which were lined up neatly on a nearby shelf.

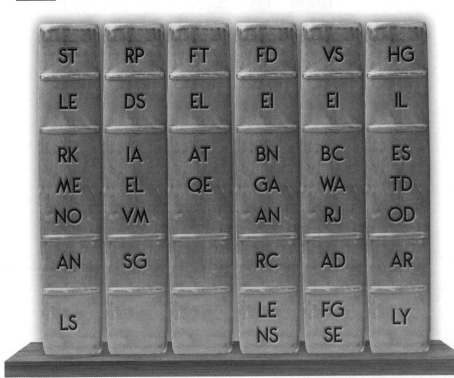

PUZZLE 144

Which book should Miss Hemmingway read?

ST LE RK ME NO AN LS

RP DS IA EL VM SG

FT EL AT QE

FD EI BN GA AN RC LE NS

VS EI BC WA RJ AD FG SE

HG IL ES TD OD AR LY

THE CURIOUS CASE OF THE CAT IN THE NIGHTTIME

HAVING SELECTED THE TITLE I REQUIRED, I carefully lifted the heavy book down from the shelf and opened it up to the most recent entry, written in impeccable penmanship. Our dear departed Father Featherby, it seemed, kept very detailed notes, many of them carefully coded. I wondered if I could find any evidence of the missing money within these inked pages…

PUZZLE 145

Father Featherby's notes are in the form of a math puzzle. Can you solve it to see the deficit in the funds?

- Withdraw 1/3 of the original petty cash for church repairs to fund the roof. - $_____.

- Use 2/3 of this amount for the labor and tiles - $500 - and keep 1/3 for contingency.

- Total church funds - $_____

- Loss - 1/3 roof funds - $_____

PUZZLE
146

3			9	8			7	
			3			1		9
					7		4	3
	6				2		3	
	1	8	4		3	9	5	
	2		7				1	
1	7		2					
	3	6			9			
	9			7	5			1

186

PUZZLEBY GAZETTE

VILLAGE NEWSLETTER

PUZZLE SECTION

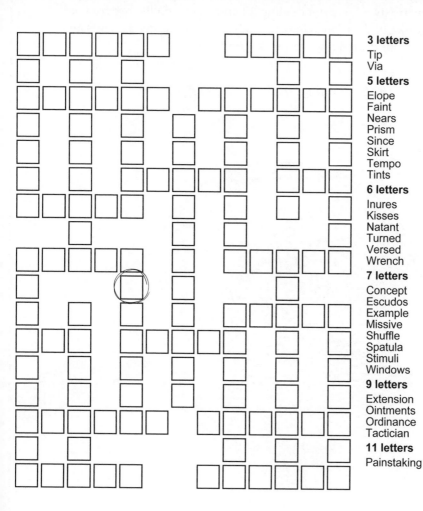

PUZZLE 147

3 letters
Tip
Via

5 letters
Elope
Faint
Nears
Prism
Since
Skirt
Tempo
Tints

6 letters
Inures
Kisses
Natant
Turned
Versed
Wrench

7 letters
Concept
Escudos
Example
Missive
Shuffle
Spatula
Stimuli
Windows

9 letters
Extension
Ointments
Ordinance
Tactician

11 letters
Painstaking

THE CURIOUS CASE OF THE CAT IN THE NIGHTTIME

FATHER FEATHERBY'S SUSPICIONS had clearly been stirred. He had even gone so far as to collect the fingerprints of all the people who regularly came in and out of the chapel. Following his line of inquiry, I took out my trusty fingerprint dusting kit and tried it on the battered old safe in the corner of the room. Unfortunately, with all the dents, scuffs and scratches, only one partial fingerprint was revealed.

Match the partial fingerprint to Father Featherby's list.

PUZZLE
148

THE CURIOUS CASE OF THE CAT IN THE NIGHTTIME

Father Featherby

Deacon Beacon

Robert Graven

Groundskeeper

Bessie Pygott

Head of Social Committee

Liza Liszt

Head of Sunday School

Caroline Adichie

Volunteer Reader

PUZZLE SECTION

PUZZLE
149

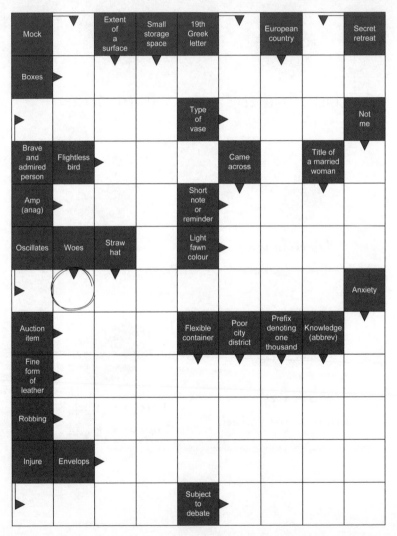

Mock		Extent of a surface	Small storage space	19th Greek letter		European country		Secret retreat
Boxes								
				Type of vase				Not me
Brave and admired person	Flightless bird				Came across		Title of a married woman	
Amp (anag)				Short note or reminder				
Oscillates	Woes	Straw hat		Light fawn colour				
								Anxiety
Auction item				Flexible container	Poor city district	Prefix denoting one thousand	Knowledge (abbrev)	
Fine form of leather								
Robbing								
Injure	Envelops							
				Subject to debate				

PUZZLEBY GAZETTE

VILLAGE NEWSLETTER

PUZZLE SECTION

PUZZLE
150

		6	8	4	9		3	
				6		7		4
							8	
		2		9				5
		3				4		
6				5		8		
	1							
9		4		7				
	6		1	2	5	3		

THE CURIOUS CASE OF THE ĈAT IN THE NIGHT TIME

THERE DIDN'T SEEM TO BE MUCH ELSE TO BE LEARNED from inside that room, so I made my way outside. There I saw Robert Graven, digging yet another grave. "Never thought I'd see the day, Miss Hemmingway, when I'd be burying Father Featherby in his own graveyard."

"It is very sad," I admitted – although I did rather feel that, at 103, one could hardly say he hadn't had a good life. I was beginning to think there wasn't much to this case at all, but I would at least try to exhaust all of the roads of inquiry before I put the matter to rest. "I don't suppose you've seen anything unusual in the grounds of the church?"

Robert scratched his chin thoughtfully. "Now you mention it, there was a disturbed patch of earth. It was on the longest path in the graveyard." He handed me an old, faded, almost unreadable map.

Solve the rectangles puzzle to find the longest path of the graveyard.

PUZZLE 151

	2		14			3			3				
22							2	2					
					6							16	
								3					
						2	14						
				7	10			5			10		
				3					9				
				6		6							2
								8					2
				3									
		5											
			20										
9								24					
							5					2	

THE CURIOUS CASE OF THE CAT IN THE NIGHTTIME

ALONG THE PATH was a row of very ancient graves, their grey stones almost entirely overgrown with thick green moss. The storm had shaken the leaves from the trees, so a heavy carpet of them covered the graveyard, hiding any disturbed dirt. I didn't like the idea of raking the whole path, so I sat on a nearby bench—dedicated to a Mr Draco Dalliance Esq—instead to take a break with a nice puzzle.

```
P  A  S  E  L  I  Z  A  B  E  T  H  S  U  E
P  L  F  U  P  R  D  U  V  N  Z  T  T  W  R
W  V  D  T  V  A  P  E  T  E  R  V  T  C  L
A  R  P  E  M  N  U  J  A  L  A  H  S  T  M
K  J  O  H  N  T  H  E  B  A  P  T  I  S  T
I  R  R  T  A  F  A  Z  R  D  S  T  R  A  S
R  A  S  I  W  O  L  E  A  G  P  P  H  D  H
H  U  O  D  L  V  N  B  H  A  Z  Z  C  U  I
W  K  T  D  S  S  T  E  A  M  H  V  S  J  M
V  V  C  H  E  A  E  L  M  Y  P  E  U  R  A
R  S  R  A  E  L  M  S  G  R  E  P  S  N  L
A  S  A  P  A  R  I  S  O  A  S  A  E  L  A
M  L  A  I  T  S  O  L  O  M  O  N  J  Q  R
A  I  L  K  I  S  I  D  A  N  J  A  C  O  B
M  G  O  F  T  H  R  A  C  H  E  L  V  H  C
```

PUZZLE
152

ABRAHAM	JACOB	MOSES	EZRA
ADAM	JESUS CHRIST	NOAH	
DELILAH	JEZEBEL	PETER	
ELIZABETH	JOHN THE BAPTIST	RACHEL	
EVE	JOSEPH	RUTH	
HEROD	JUDAS	SAMSON	
ISAAC	MARY MAGDALENE	SOLOMON	

PUZZLEBY GAZETTE

VILLAGE NEWSLETTER

**PUZZLE
153**

	P		D								
M	I	L	I	E			E			A	
	N		F		A		I		E		
S	E	L			F	E	R		E	N	C
			E		F		S				
	E	R	R		R			L	E	A	M
	L		E		D			E			
P	O	I	N	T				A	S	H	E	D
	Q		T			P		S			
	U	D	I	C	I	A	L		N	E	C	K
	E		A		P		I		E		L
I		S	T	E			F	U	S	I	O	N
	T		E		Y		Y		S		T

A B C D E F G H I J K L M N O P Q R S T U V W X Y Z

194

PUZZLE
154

					4			
						4	9	1
7	1	4						5
5	6				9			3
		9	2			6		
3								
	9	8	5	3		1		

195

THE CURIOUS CASE OF THE CAT IN THE NIGHTTIME

I SCRAPED AWAY THE LEAVES, and there indeed was a patch of
dirt, recently disturbed. There was a little trowel nearby for neatening
up the graves. I was sure Robert wouldn't mind if I borrowed it. Curiously, I
found, not the missing money, but some broken up garbage. Feeling quite the
archaeologist, I dug up whatever I could.

**PUZZLE
138**

*What did Miss Hemmingway discover?
Write your findings below.*

THE CURIOUS CASE OF THE CAT IN THE NIGHTTIME

AS I PEERED DOWN AT THE SHATTERED CHINA — so pretty it had been a crime to crack it — I noticed something else: footprints in the slippery mud, leading away to the back of the chapel. Several people seemed to have walked the path, but I found the individual prints quite easy to distinguish.

Match the footprints to their owners.

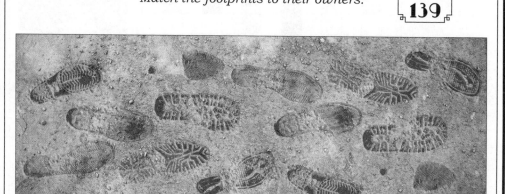

Findings:

Father Featherby	Deacon Beacon	Lisa Liszt Head of Sunday School	Robert Graven Groundskeeper	D.C. Copper	Bessie Pygott Head of Social Committee

PUZZLE SECTION

PUZZLE
157

ARE YOU GOING DOWN
A DANGEROUS PATH
IN LIFE?
Could hidden pitfalls
be littering the way?
If you want to avoid
certain death, a discreet
consultation with Achillia
Headland is advised. Make
an appointment to have
your fortune told before
it's too late at 133 Wisteria
Avenue.

Across

1 Sea rescue vessel (8)
5 Plant used for flavouring (4)
9 Poisonous (5)
10 Removes the lid (5)
11 Device for making coffee (10)
14 Novice (6)
15 On a ship or train (6)
17 Act of making known (10)
20 Loud metallic sound (5)
21 Domestic cat (5)
22 Tune (4)
23 Dishes that begin a meal (8)

Down

1 Thin strip of wood (4)
2 Cunning (4)
3 Study of microorganisms (12)
4 Join or fasten (6)
6 Final (8)
7 Straddle (8)
8 Fellow plotter (12)
12 Manufactures (8)
13 One who steers a boat (8)
16 Agreement (6)
18 Having inherent ability (4)
19 Extras (cricket) (4)

PUZZLEBY GAZETTE
VILLAGE NEWSLETTER

PUZZLE SECTION

PUZZLE 158

3 letters
Boa
Cot
Egg
Hem
Lye
Own

4 letters
Ease
Iced
Sari
Sunk
Tire
Wind

6 letters
Damsel
Impels

7 letters
Enabled
Isomers
Praises
Surgeon

8 letters
Appeaser
Cleaning
Creditor
Disprove
Literati
Travails

9 letters
Allocated
Limousine
Schoolboy
Suggested

10 letters
Digression
Elliptical
Monumental
Reflective

THE CURIOUS CASE OF THE CAT IN THE NIGHTTIME

DEEP IN THOUGHT, I hurried back home to the comfort of my winged armchair and a rich dessert. While indulging in my slice of cherry cake, I noticed the plate looked somewhat familiar. I polished off my pudding and found the other plates that had been dropped off by people around town. (I made no secret of my fondness for sweet treats, and often received a bakery's worth of cake for my birthday!)

One was a perfect match.

PUZZLE 159

What is the house number of the most likely suspect? Which plate do the broken fragments match?

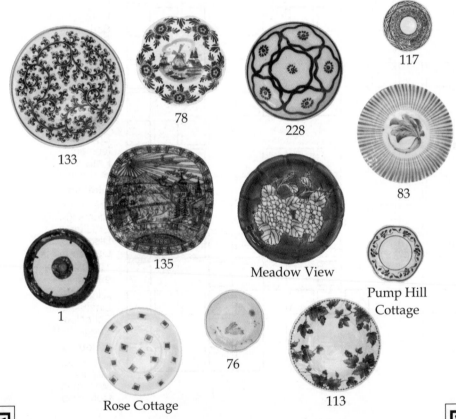

133

78

228

117

135

Meadow View

83

1

Pump Hill Cottage

Rose Cottage

76

113

THE CURIOUS CASE OF THE CAT IN THE NIGHTTIME

JUST THEN, I heard the clang of the mailbox snapping shut. When I entered the hallway, I saw a note had been shoved through the door. Before I could snatch it up, however, Baskerville tore it into pieces in a fit of mischievous exuberance.

"Bad dog," I shouted at him—though I could never stay angry at him for long. Besides, perhaps I could piece the note back together...

Piece the note back together to discover the message.

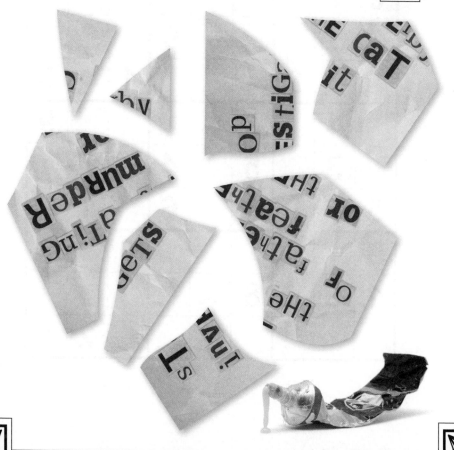

PUZZLE
161

6	7							
					9		8	7
		8				1		5
	4		3					9
	3		5		4		7	
5					6		1	
9		4				8		
1	5		8					
							2	1

PUZZLEBY GAZETTE
VILLAGE NEWSLETTER

PUZZLE SECTION

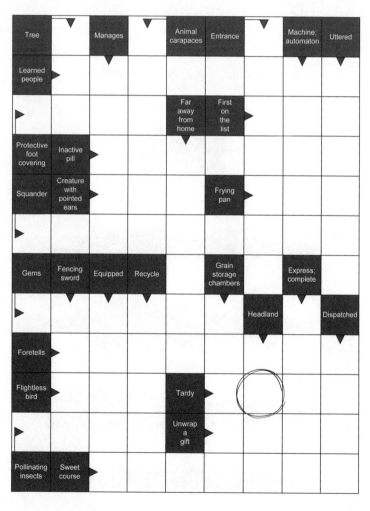

The crossword clues visible in the grid:

- Tree
- Manages
- Animal carapaces
- Entrance
- Machine; automaton
- Uttered
- Learned people
- Far away from home
- First on the list
- Protective foot covering
- Inactive pill
- Squander
- Creature with pointed ears
- Frying pan
- Gems
- Fencing sword
- Equipped
- Recycle
- Grain storage chambers
- Express; complete
- Headland
- Dispatched
- Foretells
- Flightless bird
- Tardy
- Unwrap a gift
- Pollinating insects
- Sweet course

THE CURIOUS CASE OF THE CAT IN THE NIGHTTIME

ALARMED, **I** CALLED **D.C. COPPER**, who came over to my
house immediately.

"Don't worry, Miss Hemmingway," he told me, patting me reassuringly
on the shoulder. "Cat will not have gone quietly—perhaps we can find his
meow on one of these recordings? I only took them an hour ago."

He produced the sound recordings from various parts of Puzzleby, which
he kept a record of in case they were needed. We listened intently to see if we
could hear my beloved Cat.

Find Cat's meow in one of the recordings below

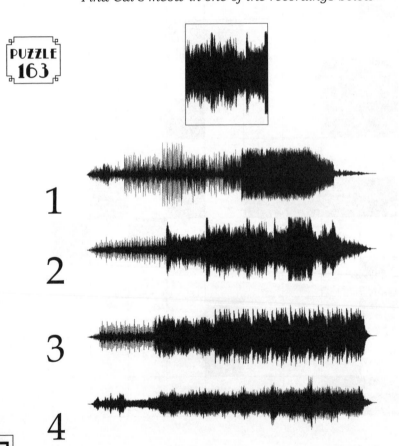

PUZZLE
163

1

2

3

4

THE CURIOUS CASE OF THE CAT IN THE NIGHTTIME

MY HEART LEAPT TO HEAR CAT MEOWING his little lungs
out in the background of one of the sounds, and I nearly fell over in
my excitement.

"There he is!" I exclaimed, pulling myself together. "Just then—did you
hear him?"

"Excellent!" grinned D.C. Copper, rewinding the piece on his clunky
recorder. "Now we just have to work out whereabouts in Puzzleby this
recording was taken…"

Make your way around the map to see where Cat was heard.

PUZZLE
164

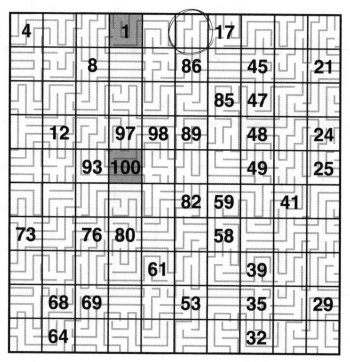

PUZZLEBY GAZETTE
VILLAGE NEWSLETTER

**PUZZLE
165**

						8		
	1		3				4	
3		5	2		4			7
	9							
		8				7		
	3	7	8					
		3						
				2		6		

PUZZLEBY GAZETTE
VILLAGE NEWSLETTER

PUZZLE SECTION

PUZZLE
166

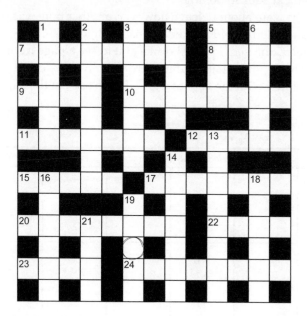

Across

7 Abandoned (8)
8 ___ Duncan Smith: politician (4)
9 Grey-haired with age (4)
10 Copycat (8)
11 Parcel (7)
12 Small woodland (5)
15 Attractive (5)
17 Concern; implicate (7)
20 Set free (8)
22 ___ Macpherson: Australian model (4)
23 Repeat an action (4)
24 Made untidy with garbage (8)

Down

1 Spanish title for a married woman (6)
2 Tall type of furry hat (8)
3 Part of an orchestra (7)
4 Mingle with something else (5)
5 ___ Minnelli: US actress (4)
6 People who fly airplanes (6)
13 Device recording distance travelled (8)
14 Turns upside down (7)
16 Voiles (anag) (6)
18 Principles (6)
19 Shopping centers (5)
21 Greek god of love (4)

THE CURIOUS CASE OF THE CAT IN THE NIGHTTIME

I **SET MY TEACUP DOWN** and stood to join D.C. Copper with my trusty hound Baskerville at my side.

"Come on, Miss Hemmingway," said the officer, straightening his hat. "We'll have Cat back in no time!"

Just as we were about to leave however, another note was pushed through the door, and I deftly held Baskerville back while D.C. Copper took it from the doormat. Confused, I peered down at it to see a page from someone's calendar. The appointments within were written in code, but one I could quickly decipher with the help of a grid on the back of the page.

Monday	Tuesday	Wednesday	Thursday	Friday	Saturday	Sunday
1/M 7/D RIGHT +2						
		9/E 15/M UP +1				
				18/Q 19/A LEFT +2		
			2/T 11/S UP +3			

THE CURIOUS CASE OF THE CAT IN THE NIGHTTIME

Decipher the code for the appointments.

	1	2	3	4	5	6	7	8	9	10	11	12	13	14	15	16	17	18	19	20
A	Z	Q	G	H	D	D	R	M	O	W	F	L	K	A	C	O	I	P	H	G
B	T	I	O	P	L	K	C	V	K	D	J	Z	A	L	Q	E	T	P	L	J
C	P	Q	B	M	F	H	Y	S	C	Q	G	Y	I	H	K	M	X	G	S	R
D	P	O	I	U	J	H	B	E	A	S	I	H	L	X	Y	B	Y	D	J	Y
E	P	E	O	H	J	K	F	R	M	S	B	J	K	F	E	E	N	H	J	K
F	Q	Z	D	V	G	N	J	K	G	Y	M	E	Q	Y	L	M	H	T	D	G
G	P	O	K	M	J	H	G	B	D	Y	T	R	S	G	R	P	O	U	B	G
H	Q	I	P	O	I	K	J	H	G	T	F	B	M	F	E	W	E	T	Y	U
I	O	I	H	G	N	X	C	V	B	N	H	K	G	F	T	W	F	N	K	L
J	Y	H	N	T	G	B	T	G	B	F	E	W	S	X	T	Q	A	Z	P	L
K	A	L	F	J	M	I	L	E	F	C	G	N	D	J	A	L	E	B	N	M
L	U	J	H	G	F	V	N	M	Y	G	F	D	S	V	H	K	J	H	G	F
M	F	Q	R	W	E	E	D	T	E	Y	R	U	I	I	C	O	K	P	S	D
N	Z	L	A	D	C	V	G	H	N	J	U	Y	T	R	U	I	O	P	D	F
O	M	N	B	V	C	X	D	G	Y	U	I	K	L	O	P	E	D	S	X	Z
P	X	D	F	Y	U	I	O	L	K	J	O	Q	S	C	V	G	H	U	J	K
Q	Y	E	D	X	C	V	G	U	I	O	L	N	L	A	J	E	G	J	F	D
R	P	O	I	U	Y	H	G	F	V	N	M	H	G	F	D	K	I	U	Y	T
S	N	H	G	F	D	Y	T	R	E	H	Y	B	V	C	X	F	Y	U	I	I
T	F	N	K	I	U	Y	H	J	M	N	B	V	G	T	R	E	D	C	B	N

....

....

....

....

PUZZLE 168

	5				7	2		
7		2		8			4	
6								
		4	6			3	8	
		6		1		9		
	8	1			2	5		
								2
	6			4		1		8
		3	1				5	

210

PUZZLEBY GAZETTE

VILLAGE NEWSLETTER

PUZZLE SECTION

PUZZLE
169

C		A	N	C	E			T		D		G
	O					M	A			E		L
A		E	L	I		E		P		R		A
	P			N		T		E		A		S
D	I	S		R	E	E				N		
	N			I		S				G		E
I	G	U	A	N	A		C	O	W	E		S
N		N		G			N			E		
				P	R	E				G		
A		U	R	E		E		U		A		
N					S	A	N	D	P	I		
C		E	X	I	S	T		C				
Y	E	T		L			A	T	T	E	S	T

A B C D E F G H I J K L M N O P Q R S T U V W X Y Z

211

THE CURIOUS CASE OF THE CAT IN THE NIGHTTIME

WITH RENEWED RESOLVE, D.C. Copper, Baskerville and I hurried to the location indicated on the map. It was around the back of the old textiles factory, and as we drew closer, I heard the distinct meowing of my beloved Cat.

Unfortunately, the towering mill building made everything echo so much that I couldn't figure out where the mewling sound was coming from! I closed my eyes and focused…

Solve the battleships puzzle to figure out where the sound is loudest.

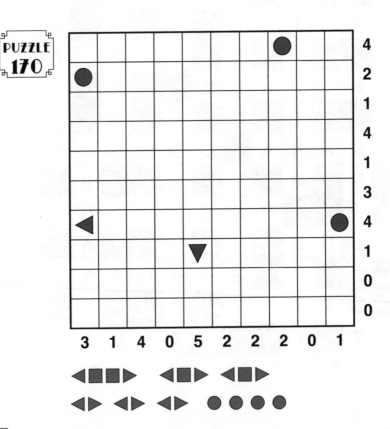

PUZZLE 170

4
2
1
4
1
3
4
1
0
0

3 1 4 0 5 2 2 2 0 1

212

THE CURIOUS CASE OF THE CAT IN THE NIGHTTIME

I **DESPERATELY SCANNED THE BUILDING** and saw three broken windows, each adorned with torn cobwebs that fluttered in the draught. But there was no debris crunching on the path beneath me—not a single shard.

How odd, I thought, contemplating the shattered shapes in the glass. I wonder if the shards that were dug up from the graveyard would match any of those holes…

Fortunately, I still had them in my handbag, so I took them out to compare against the window.

Match the shards of glass to the broken window.

PUZZLE
171

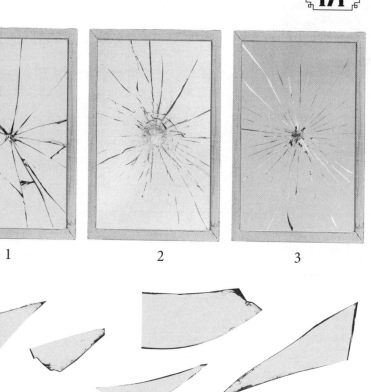

1   2   3

PUZZLE SECTION

PUZZLE 172

A stunning eclipse graced our skies this week. However, it occurred on the Capricorn/Cancer axis, which prompts us to consider how safe and secure we feel in life. Some may wish to turn to faith to deal with this, others to facts and logic. Don't let these feelings push you into tiptoeing around, however; sometimes you just have to deal with them head-on.

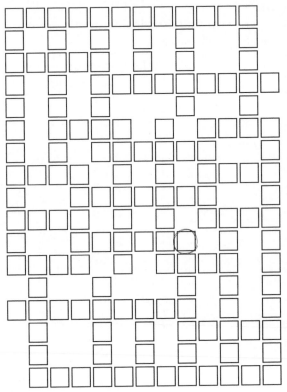

4 letters
Acne
Ante
Aria
Diet
Dole
Drat
Iced
Idle
Nets
Sets

5 letters
Deans
Evens
Noisy
Oribi
Steed
Venom

6 letters
Eraser
Gyrate
Locate
Nodded

7 letters
Combing
Dragoon
Eyelids
Vacated
Villain

8 letters
Exterior
Ignorant

9 letters
Beefsteak
Hamstring

12 letters
Civilisation
Coincidental
Rhododendron
Transmission

PUZZLE
173

6	15	22	15	12	12	25	12		2	15	4	25
	26		1		23		11		19		1	
19	15	5	5	23	9		10	25	11	8	25	1
	12		12		24	25	15		25		25	
3	11	1	25		25		12	23	14	25	12	10
	1			1					25			
13	25	24	25	22	9		7	15	22	22	25	13
			8				25				1	
9	24	22	17	1	5		9		16	17	15	10
	11		12		15	18	24		17		26	
11	20	24	15	23	12		25	13	23	26	12	25
	23		24		25		22		24		25	
15	21	22	25		9	17	9	6	25	1	9	25

A B C D E F G H I J K L M N O P Q R S T U V W X Y Z

1	2	3	4	5	6	7	8	9	10	11	12	13
									Y			

14	15	16	17	18	19	20	21	22	23	24	25	26
		Q			H							

215

THE CURIOUS CASE OF THE CAT IN THE NIGHTTIME

ONCE INSIDE, WE MADE OUR WAY through the corridors in the old factory. It wasn't a pleasant atmosphere; it was dark and dingy inside, with rusty, dripping pipes, moss-covered walls, and the odd fragment of graffiti.

"Little rascals," muttered D.C. Copper, running his long index finger along a name carved into the brick. "I'll have to up patrols around here!"

"There will be time for that later," I told him. "We need to finish this case first and get Cat back before any harm comes to him!"

"Right you are, Miss Hemmingway!" said the policeman, tipping his head towards me in acknowledgement. He shone his flashlight ahead of us, scouring the floor for any obstacles.

Unfortunately, the corridor network was a maze, and the vandals hadn't included any directions in their graffiti. We had to navigate carefully through the gloom, hopping over puddles and ducking beneath thick cobwebs.

THE CURIOUS CASE OF THE CAT IN THE NIGHTTIME

Figure out the route through the maze to guide Miss Hemmingway, D.C. Copper and Baskerville to Cat.

PUZZLE 175

In favor of		Peer	William ___: famous playwright	Deep anger		Opposite of an acid		Goal
Repress								
				Deciduous tree				Affirmative vote
Ark builder	Piece of cloth				Prevent		Dance	
Kind or sort				Young child				
Landing and take-off area	Unit of length	Make less dense		___ vera: used in cosmetics				
								Youngsters aged from 13 - 19
Short sleep				Lyric poem	Cloth worn around the waist	Where darts players throw from	At that time	
Wood preserver								
Nuisance; unpleasant problem								
Island of the Inner Hebrides	Revive; renew							
				Female chickens				

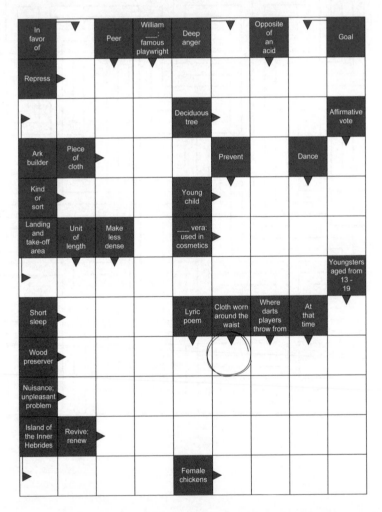

PUZZLE SECTION

			6		4			
		3			8		2	
7	5					9		
		5	1				9	
		2		5		3		
	8				3	2		
		7					1	6
	2		4			5		
			9		7			

PUZZLE
176

219

ON OUR WAY DOWN ONE PARTICULARLY gloomy corridor, Baskerville pulled slightly to the left, snuffling noisily at what I discovered to be a messy pile of discarded paper. Upon closer inspection, I found a page of a diary, on which an entry had been written in a strange picture code.

"What have you got there?" asked D.C. Copper, peering over my shoulder, but I was already reading intently.

THE CURIOUS CASE OF THE CAT IN THE NIGHTTIME

A SHOCK RAN THROUGH ME as I realized that I had been missing the bigger picture all along. Could all these murders be connected? I wondered, forehead furrowing as I contemplated the idea. Baskerville was sitting at my feet, his wagging tail casting more shadows over the walls. Shuffling the papers in my hands, I found another piece of paper, also written in a code. I quickly decoded it to discover another clue.

Use the code to reveal a hidden message.

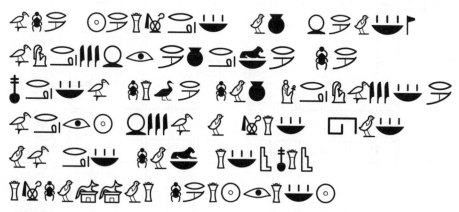

PUZZLE
177

PUZZLE
178

Solve the code to reveal another clue.

NBAANSA
OROSOTPD
ALBLNENDO
KPIFCTRHO

PUZZLE SECTION

PUZZLE
179

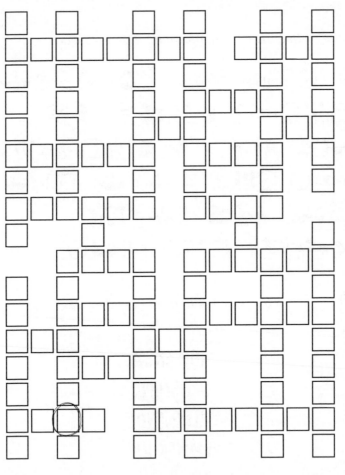

3 letters
Arm
Ash
Lug
Sag
She
Was

4 letters
Aura
Chic
Magi
Nine
Nosy
Orca
Ties
Zeta

6 letters
Aplomb
Crease
Delete
Haggis

7 letters
Bowline
Garages

8 letters
Adoption
Chastens
Classify
Convulse
Flamingo
Greeting
Hideaway
Legality
Uncommon
Zimbabwe

9 letters
Aspersion
Matriarch

PUZZLEBY GAZETTE
VILLAGE NEWSLETTER

Across

1 Republic once ruled by Idi Amin (6)
7 Pestered constantly (8)
8 Nevertheless (3)
9 George ___ : composer (6)
10 Suggestion; thought (4)
11 Small heron (5)
13 Rearranged letters of a word (7)
15 Obedient (7)
17 Lure an animal into a trap (5)
21 Delude (4)
22 End a dispute (6)
23 Mixture of gases we breathe (3)
24 Range of colors (8)
25 At sixes and ___ : in disarray (6)

Down

1 Refined in manner (6)
2 Part of a stamen (6)
3 Live by (5)
4 Confusing (7)
5 Item of sweet food (8)
6 Former Spanish currency (6)
12 Proof of something (8)
14 People who manage college finances (7)
16 Takes the place of (6)
18 Make (6)
19 Yearns for (6)
20 Plant stalks (5)

THE CURIOUS CASE OF THE CAT IN THE NIGHTTIME

WE TOOK A FEW MORE TENTATIVE steps forward under the flickering lights. My next step brought my foot uncomfortably into contact with a tin box, which jangled rather musically as it went skidding across the floor. D.C. Copper kindly picked it up for me and pried it open.

"This must be the missing funds from the church!" he cried, but before I could remind him to be quiet, I heard a distinctive meowing coming from close by. I hurried around the corner and discovered my feline friend hiding behind one of the pipes in the corridor beyond.

"There you are!" D.C. Copper said happily as I bent down to pat Cat on his furry head. "Righto, let's get back and pop the kettle on."

The policeman started back in the direction from where we'd come, but Cat started urgently pawing at another door with a three-digit code on the heavy padlock.

Solve the sudoku to find the code for the lock.

PUZZLE
181

			1		4	2		8
8	O		6					
				2			7	1
		4				8	O	5
	3			O			2	
1		9				3		
7	1			5				
					7			6
3		2	9		8			

THE CURIOUS CASE OF THE CAT IN THE NIGHTTIME

I WAS NOW QUITE SURE THAT, behind this door, I would discover the mastermind behind all the murders that have been plaguing Puzzleby. Before I opened it, I took a moment to assess what I knew so far…

KNOWNS AND UNKNOWNS

The mastermind met with each of the murderers before the victims were killed.

☐ True   ☐ Not true   ☐ Unknown

The Deacon was embezzling funds meant for the church roof.

☐ True   ☐ Not true   ☐ Unknown

The Deacon refused to have his fortune told.

☐ True   ☐ Not true   ☐ Unknown

Did you decode the message from *The Puzzleby Gazette*?

_ _ _ _ , _ _ !   _ _ _ _ _ _ _ _   _ _ _ _ _ _ _ _ _ _   _ _   _ _   _ _ _ _ _ _ _

Write the name of your main suspect below:

THE CURIOUS CASE OF THE CAT IN THE NIGHTTIME

BEHIND THE DOOR WAS A WALL plastered with newspaper clippings and scraps of scrawled notes. Photographs of the recent victims and their killers stared down at me, each connected with thin red string. And standing in front of it all was Dahliah Dalliance.

"Miss Hemmingway," she sneered. "I wasn't expecting you to catch up to me, let alone so quickly."

"You underestimated me," I replied. "And now you're finished— you won't be able to mastermind any more murders."

"It was an ingenious plan," Dahliah lamented. "Writing doesn't pay what it used to, so I picked up the fortune telling business on the side. Then I realized—if I could find a good murder, I could add some excitement to my novels and make a name for myself in the thriller genre!"

"You put the idea into the murderers' heads when they came to you to have their fortunes told," I realized. "That way, you didn't have to do any of your own dirty work."

"You were too smart for me, Miss Hemmingway," Dahliah grumbled.

"Oh, I didn't do it alone," I smiled. "I had some help. Someone was hiding clues in the newspaper puzzles…"

With perfect timing, the door behind me creaked open and Deirdre Dalliance entered, much to the surprise of her mother.

"I hid messages in the newspapers to Miss Hemmingway to help her," she explained. "I had to stop you, Mom."

"Deirdre! How could you?" gasped Dahliah, just as D.C. Copper returned.

"Well done, Miss Hemmingway," he said, withdrawing a pair of silver handcuffs. He arrested Dahliah and she was led out of the room, protesting all the way. Deirdre shuffled after them, her mousy head bowed.

Cat leapt up into my arms, Baskerville wagging his tail happily at my side.

"Well then," I said, looking at my faithful companions. "Time for a cup of tea, I think!"

THE CURIOUS CASE OF THE CAT IN THE NIGHTTIME

ALL'S WELL THAT ENDS WELL, I thought, settling down in front of the fire with Baskerville and Cat. I put my cup of tea down on the side table and carefully balanced a piece of shortbread in my lap.

"Right then," I said to my companions, flipping open the newspaper and taking out a pen. "Time for one last puzzle before bed…"

N	P	A	G	C	D	E	T	E	L	P	E	D	O	L
A	R	S	C	O	R	E	D	A	X	I	K	P	L	E
O	D	A	O	C	L	O	S	E	D	D	O	W	N	S
E	Q	E	D	I	O	T	Y	A	P	J	J	C	F	K
F	R	A	I	E	S	M	R	H	E	P	H	U	I	T
W	P	S	E	T	H	S	P	L	X	C	O	R	N	E
D	U	D	A	D	P	C	E	L	N	S	R	T	I	R
E	D	G	E	E	P	M	N	R	I	T	O	A	S	M
N	E	C	N	D	E	X	E	I	S	S	S	I	H	I
I	P	W	O	U	N	D	U	P	L	K	H	N	E	N
A	P	O	P	L	P	E	R	F	E	C	T	E	D	A
R	A	X	K	C	O	M	P	L	E	T	E	D	D	T
D	R	W	U	N	H	G	O	T	I	T	D	O	N	E
R	W	R	A	O	S	T	O	Q	O	P	R	F	I	D
I	B	D	A	C	H	I	E	V	E	D	T	F	U	S

ACCOMPLISHED	CURTAINED-OFF	LAST STAGE
ACHIEVED	DEPLETED	PERFECTED
CEASED	DRAINED	SCORED
CLINCHED	EMPTIED	STOPPED
CLOSED DOWN	ENDED	TERMINATED
COMPLETED	FINISHED	WOUND UP
CONCLUDED	GOT IT DONE	WRAPPED UP

ANSWERS

If you're stuck, Miss Hemmingway has kindly shared her answers...

1

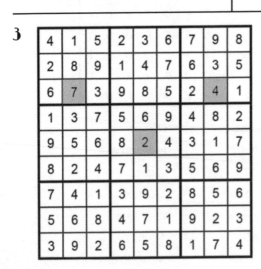

2

The letters spell out
**WHY DO BEES
ATTACK?**

3

4	1	5	2	3	6	7	9	8
2	8	9	1	4	7	6	3	5
6	7	3	9	8	5	2	4	1
1	3	7	5	6	9	4	8	2
9	5	6	8	2	4	3	1	7
8	2	4	7	1	3	5	6	9
7	4	1	3	9	2	8	5	6
5	6	8	4	7	1	9	2	3
3	9	2	6	5	8	1	7	4

ANSWERS

4

50	51	53	55	56	62	63	64	65	66
49	52	54	57	61	87	86	70	69	67
29	48	58	60	88	89	90	85	71	68
28	30	47	59	98	99	96	91	84	72
16	27	31	46	100	97	95	92	83	73
15	17	26	32	45	94	93	82	79	74
7	14	18	25	33	44	81	80	78	75
6	8	13	19	24	34	43	77	76	40
2	5	9	12	20	23	35	42	41	39
1	3	4	10	11	21	22	36	37	38

5

6

Crossword solution grid:

Row: E R B
Row: T A C I T U R N
Row: M A N — F I N — O
Row: T — F A G I N
Row: U S E S — R A S P
Row: P — B A L S A
Row: M A S T — O U R
Row: P — S — W E T
Row: A L L A Y — I
Row: B A I L — B U S
Row: L I S Z T — A M A
Row: H A Y — T A N

7

The missing number in Frederick's doodle is "6", as each row and column adds up to 11.

Therefore, since the phone numbers are in the order of those rows, Miss Hemmingway needs to phone Lisa Liszt.

ANSWERS

8

4	7	(2)	6	1	5	8	9	3
8	1	9	3	5	7	2	4	6
3	6	5	2	8	4	9	1	7
7	9	6	4	3	2	5	8	1
5	2	8	1	6	9	7	3	4
2	3	7	8	9	1	4	6	5
9	4	1	5	7	6	3	2	8
6	5	3	9	4	8	1	7	2
1	8	4	7	2	3	6	5	9

9

Kakuro solution with filled cells:

8	7			9	1
1	9	8	4	1	2
1	2	9	3	4	2
9	8	7	2	1	
	8	7	3	2	1
8	9	5	7	9	8
8	9	2	1	3	4
9	6	8	9	7	
	2	3	2	3	1
8	7	9	3	2	3
3	1	2	4	3	1
8	9		1	2	

10

The above matches:

3-methylbutyl acetate (bananas)

ANSWERS

11

A	B	L	E		S	T	A	P	L	E	R	S
L		E		I		H		E	X		A	
A	D	V	A	N	C	E		N	I	P	P	Y
R		E		C		O		N		R		S
M	A	L	N	O	U	R	I	S	H	E	D	
I		N		Y		Y		S		S		B
S	T	A	R	V	E		E	L	I	S	H	A
T		M		E		T		V		S		N
	F	A	I	N	T	H	E	A	R	T	E	D
E		D		I		R		N		R		A
T	H	E	R	E		U	N	I	T	I	N	G
C		U		N		S		A		C		E
H	E	S	I	T	A	T	E		W	E	N	D

12

	C	H	I	V	E		O	S	I	E	R
G		Y		A		J		H		R	E
R	E	P	U	L	S	E		E	X	A	L	T
I		O		E		E		A			C
L	O	C	K		A	P	P	R	O	A	C	H
L		R		M		S		E			N
E	L	I	X	I	R		C	R	U	T	C	H
		S		S		B		S		I		O
A	N	Y	W	H	E	R	E		A	Q	U	A
D				M		I		D		U		R
Z	E	B	R	A		E	M	E	R	A	L	D
E		A		S		F		N		R		S
	I	T	C	H	Y		S	T	A	Y	S

13

877 + 877 = 1754

Phone number:
877 877 1754

14

ANSWERS

15

	4	12			17	9	
10	3	7		17/19	9	8	19
3	1	2	25/24	9	7	1	8	11
	14	3	8	2	1	7	9	8
16/18		9	8	6/6	1	2	3
24	9	8	7	5/14	3	2	7
16	7	9	24/10	3	1	4	2	5
	14	1	7	4	2	9/4	1	3
9/14		9	7	7/16	1	4	2
24	7	9	8	10/5	2	3	13
5	2	3	11/14	2	3	5	4	12
	10	2	3	1	4	17	8	9
		15	8	7		4	1	3

(8 is circled)

16

	I		C					C
I	N	D	E	P	T	H		L
	V		L		R	O	P	E
M	A	C	A	D	A	M	I	A
	D	A	D		Y	E	A	R
H	E	R	O	N		O	N	E
	D		N			S	I	R
		S		B	I	T	S	
A	U	K		U		A	S	K
R	I	M	S		S	I	N	
G		R	E	G	I	M	E	
S	E	U	S	S		S	O	W

(A in MACADAMIA is circled)

17

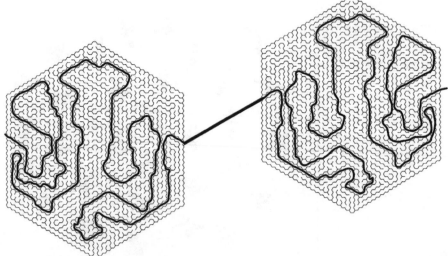

ANSWERS

18

```
  C   S   P   S   H       S
B O O K M A R K   O A T S
  L   E   Y   U   O   Y X
C U R L   L A N D F I L L
  M   E   O   K       E
I N S T E A D   L O R D S
  O   D   T   V       R
F U N N Y   B R E E Z E S
  N   C   A   R       N
S W A N S O N G   D I M E
  E   U   S   E   O   E
C L A M   T I D I N E S S
  L   B   S   Y   E   H
```

19

4	1	3	7	6	9	8	2	5
7	8	5	2	3	4	6	1	9
9	2	6	1	8	5	4	3	7
2	7	4	8	5	3	1	9	6
8	6	1	9	2	7	5	4	3
5	3	9	6	4	1	7	8	2
6	(5)	2	4	9	8	3	7	1
1	9	8	3	7	6	2	5	4
3	4	7	5	1	2	9	6	8

20

LEMON DROPS

STRAWBERRY JELLY

VANILLA ICE CREAM

CAT FOOD

DANISH PASTRY

GINGERBREAD

PAIN AU CHOCOLAT

PEANUT BUTTER

21

CHERRIES

POTATOES

EGGS

SARDINES

BANANAS

SCONES

APPLES

WENSLEYDALE

22

6	1	3	9	2	5	4	8	7
4	9	8	1	7	3	2	6	5
7	2	5	3	6	9	8	1	4
8	7	6	4	5	2	1	3	9
2	3	9	5	1	4	6	7	8
1	6	4	8	3	7	9	5	2
3	4	1	7	9	8	5	2	6
5	8	2	6	4	1	7	9	3
9	5	7	2	8	6	3	4	1

23

						T		U
D	R	A	M	A		O	W	N
	I	V	A	N		M		S
	P	O	R	T	H	O	L	E
	P	I	G		A	R	I	A
S	I	D	E	B	U	R	N	S
	N				L	O	G	O
E	G	G	S			W	O	N
		L	U	K	E			A
	Y	U	A	N		L	A	B
	O	V	E	R	A	L	L	
R	E	N	E	W		G	E	E

ANSWERS

24

File 39 belongs to the beekeeper.

25

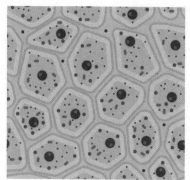

Bee venom

26

27

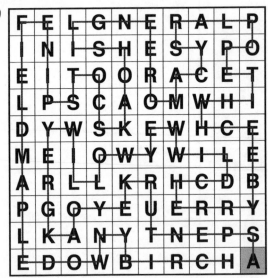

28

J. Willis
F. Bailey
D. Dalliance
F. Jones
L. Luck

29

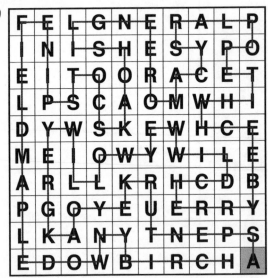

"Ash" is the missing word.

ANSWERS

30

31

32

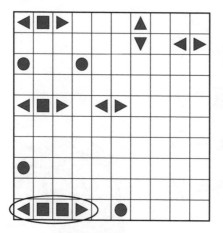

This area contains the most bees.

CRIME 1 CONCLUSIONS

John the Beekeeper was allergic to bees. – True

Liza Liszt visited John on the day of his death. – Unknown

The smell of an angry bee's pheromones is the same as rotten apples. – Not true.

Frederick Bailey might have known of John's allergy. – True

The message hidden in *The Puzzleby Gazette* is "Bees hate banana".

The killer is Fredrick Bailey.

33

3	5	6	4	9	8	2	7	1
4	2	7	3	5	1	8	6	9
8	1	9	2	6	7	5	3	4
7	4	8	1	3	9	6	5	2
6	9	2	7	8	5	4	1	3
5	3	1	6	4	2	9	8	7
9	7	4	8	1	6	3	2	5
2	8	3	5	7	4	1	9	6
1	6	5	9	2	3	7	4	8

34

1. MACK CHATTERLEY

2. AMBROSE ATKINSON

3. JACQUES BROCHET

4. CLEMENTINE COTTON

5. IRENE COTTON

Jacques is the victim.

35

$$\blacklozenge - \blacklozenge = 0$$

$$\bullet - \blacksquare = 1$$

$$\blacksquare + \blacktriangle = 3$$

$$\blacktriangle \times \blacklozenge = 7$$

ANSWERS

36

The word scramble spells "MEET AT THE LAKE AT MIDNIGHT".

37

	A		D			D		
	G	R	E	Y	N	E	S	S
H	E	I	R			L	I	T
		V	I	B	R	A	T	O
		E	V	E		Y	A	W
I	N	T	E	R	F	E	R	E
			E		D			D
T	I	P	O	F	F		A	
	N	E	U	T	R	A	L	S
	C	A	T			O	N	T	O
H	E	L	D			S	T	A	B
		S	O	R	T	E	R	S

38

1	8	9	5	7	3	6	4	2
3	6	7	2	9	4	5	1	8
5	2	4	8	6	1	7	3	9
9	7	2	4	1	5	3	8	6
4	5	1	6	3	8	2	9	7
8	3	6	7	2	9	4	5	1
2	1	5	9	4	7	8	6	3
6	9	8	3	5	2	1	7	4
7	4	3	1	8	6	9	2	5

39

Alcohol = Positive.

40

The close-up image is of nylon

41

ANSWERS

42

```
WANDER   DOUSED
 R   A   O    R    T  O
SKILLS   UNVEIL
 Q   L   EBB       A  L
 U   I          A  M  I
 (I)MPACTS   PISTE
 R   N   I    A    H  S
 T   C      CHI    H  I
STEER        RAPID
     F   USE       U  D
 C   F   N    P    T  IS
OVERS    OCTOPUS
 U   C   C    P       E
 L   T   THE       I  N
OCULAR   AFLOAT
 M   A   I    R    O  C
BOLERO   NOTATE
```

43

Kakuro solution grid (partial readings):

```
              9   18          24  16
      3   2   1   18      16   9   7
     18
      30  8   7   9   6    17   8   9
  9                    6
  3   2   1   26  8   9   2   7
 24              11
      7   9   8    4   3   1      18  3
              6
           5 (2   3) 24 (3   1   2)
     15            8       10
  4   17  6   1   2   8        9   1
      4                    19
  4   3   1   19  1   7   3   8
         10
 11   1   8   2   16  9   7
                  13          14  11
          4   3   1   24  9   7   8
     11            11       4
 11   1   5   3   2   10  1   3
16                         10
      9   7   30  9   8   7   6
 5                 4
      2   3        4   1   3
```

44

38	39	41	42	75	76	85	86	96	95
37	40	43	74	77	84	87	97	**100**	94
36	44	45	73	78	83	88	99	98	93
22	35	46	72	79	82	89	91	92	66
21	23	34	47	71	80	81	90	67	65
11	20	24	33	48	70	69	68	64	63
10	12	19	25	32	49	60	61	62	57
4	9	13	18	26	31	50	59	58	56
3	5	8	14	17	27	30	51	55	54
1	2	6	7	15	16	28	29	52	53

45

9	4	6	5	7	8	1	3	2
2	3	1	7	5	6	8	9	4
8	7	4	9	3	2	6	5	1
1	2	5	6	4	3	9	7	8
4	6	8	1	9	7	3	2	5
3	5	9	8	2	1	7	4	6
5	8	2	3	1	9	4	6	7
6	9	7	2	8	4	5	1	3
7	1	3	4	6	5	2	8	9

46

		C							R
W	O	O		E	N	S	U		E
	F	L	O	R	E	T			V
A	F	T		A	G	A	T	E	
		S		S	A	V	E	R	
	H		T			T	E	A	S
L	A	I	R			I	D	L	E
	I		I		O				D
B	R	A	N	D	N	E	W		
	D	U	K	E		C	O	L	
T	O	K	E	N		H	O	E	
	S	T	Y			O	D	E	

47

3: D. C.
Copper

2: Wellington
Boots

ANSWERS

48

49

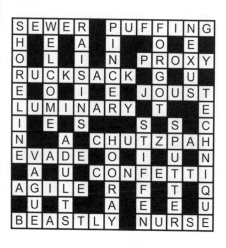

```
S E W E R   P U F F I N G
H   E   A   I     O   E
O   L   I   N   P R O X Y
R U C K S A C K   G   U
E   O   I   E   J O U S T
L U M I N A R Y   T     E
I   E   S       S   S   C
N   A   C H U T Z P A H   H
E V A D E   O   I   U   N
  A   U   C O N F E T T I
A G I L E   R   F   T   Q
  U   T   A   E   E   U
B E A S T L Y   N U R S E
```

50

8	3	2	6	⑨	5	4	7	1
4	6	5	3	1	7	9	2	8
9	1	7	4	2	8	3	6	5
6	2	4	1	7	3	5	8	9
5	9	3	8	6	2	1	4	7
7	8	1	9	5	4	6	3	2
3	5	6	7	8	9	2	1	4
2	4	8	5	3	1	7	9	6
1	7	9	2	4	6	8	5	3

51

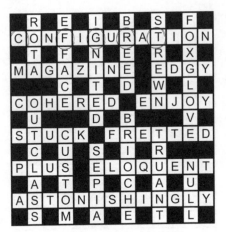

The plate is CF96 GRT

52

The car could belong to either Irene Cotton or Mack Chatterley.

53

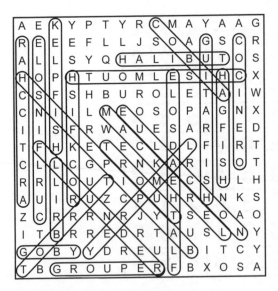

54

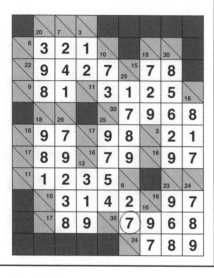

	20	7	3					
6	3	2	1	10		18	30	
22	9	4	2	7	15 / 25	7	8	
9	8	1	11	3	1	2	5	16
	18	29		30 / 25	7	9	6	8
16	9	7	17	9	8	3	2	1
17	8	9	16 / 13	7	9	16	9	7
11	1	2	3	5	9		23	24
	10	3	1	4	2	16 / 16	9	7
	17	8	9	30	7	9	6	8
					24	7	8	9

55 ICE and RUM were stolen.

	A		S			H		
	R	E	T	R	E	A	T	S
S	E	A	R			L	A	P
		T	O	B	A	C	C	O
		E	K	E		Y	O	U
I	N	N	E	R	M	O	S	T
			E		N			S
L	I	G	H	T	S		A	
	F	R	O	S	T	I	N	G
	F	U	R		A	R	G	O
D	Y	E	D		R	O	L	L
		L	E	A	R	N	E	D

56

Mack Chatterley

57

8	4	5	2	6	7	1	9	3
1	6	9	5	4	3	7	8	2
7	3	2	1	8	9	6	4	5
2	7	3	4	9	8	5	6	1
4	1	6	7	5	2	9	3	8
9	5	8	6	3	1	2	7	4
3	9	1	8	2	6	4	5	7
6	2	4	3	7	5	8	1	9
5	8	7	9	1	4	3	2	6

58

```
R O T S   D I C A P R I O
E   R   H   N   L   E   V
L E O P A R D   P A S S E
A   L   P   I   H   I   R
T U L I P   G R A N D M A
I     Y   O   N   U   M
O L D A G E   S U P E R B
N   I   O   T   M     I
S A V E L O Y   E L I O T
H   I   U   C   R   D   I
I O N I C   O R I N O C O
P   E   K   O   C   L   U
S P R A Y I N G   A S K S
```

59

15

60

10 fish are left,
since none can
leave the tank.

61

2	1	6	7	(15)	16	28	29	30	31
3	5	8	14	17	27	38	37	33	32
4	9	13	18	26	41	40	39	36	34
10	12	19	25	42	43	44	45	46	35
11	20	24	72	73	74	75	76	48	47
21	23	71	92	91	82	81	79	77	49
22	70	96	95	93	90	83	80	78	50
67	69	97	98	94	89	86	84	57	51
66	68	99	100	88	87	85	58	56	52
65	64	63	62	61	60	59	55	54	53

62

ANSWERS

63

PIKE	3 lb
CARP	2 lb
PERCH	5 lb
TROUT	39 lb
ROACH	1 lb
CATFISH	6 lb

64

4	8	6	5	7	1	9	2	3
1	9	5	4	2	3	7	6	8
7	3	2	9	5	6	1	8	4
6	7	1	3	9	8	2	4	5
9	4	8	6	1	2	3	5	7
2	5	3	8	4	7	6	1	9
5	2	9	7	6	4	8	3	1
3	1	4	2	8	9	5	7	6
8	6	7	1	3	5	4	9	2

65

66

```
P L A Y   S T A M P I N G
H   L   C U E   L     R
E N T R A N T   D E L T A
A   A   L   U   I     F
S E R I A L   T A R I F F
A       M   V   T   N   I
N E C T A R I N E   V A T
T   O   R   N     O   I
    U N I V E R S A L
S   T     G   L   V   A
E M U   R E A D I N E S S
A   R   E   R   P     S
W I E L D S   U P T A K E
A       D   S   E   Z M
T A B L E   P E R T U R B
E   O   N   A   Y   R L
R E A S S E R T   B E V Y
```

67

68

```
A M H A I G D E S E
U A S I L A W A A T
S H D N V L D R M R
T R E O E A S S L E
I I S T R R A E C
N L P M A N W O R U
S T A X W E W H T R
U I T R A T A R K B
C A M I L S T T O C
H E T H L O W E N S
```

ANSWERS

69

E	T	H	I	C	S		S	E	E	K	E	R
R		O		R		C		C		I		E
S	E	L	F	I	S	H		H		W		P
A		O		E		O	X	I	D	I	S	E
T	I	G	E	R		R		D		S		A
Z		R		E		E		N	A	S	A	L
		A		V	I	O	L	A		Q		
R	U	M	B	A		G				U		P
I		R		R		R		B	R	I	B	E
P	E	T	U	N	I	A		I		R		R
E		W		I		P	Y	J	A	M	A	S
D	I	N	G	H	Y		B	U	R	D	E	N

70

The word scramble spells "OVER YOUR DEAD BODY"

71

CRIME 2 CONCLUSIONS

Clementine and Irene Cotton read Jacques Brochet's notebook. – Not true

Mack Chatterley's motor car was spotted leaving the scene of the crime. – True

Billy Mead saw Jacques Brochet at The Murdered Pint on the night of his death. – Not true

Jacques Brochet could not swim. – Unknown.

The message hidden in *The Puzzleby Gazette* is "The missing doorstop".

The killer is Mack Chatterley.

ANSWERS

72

```
R L L O B E D E I   V Y I U O N
T F V A I A V S D A T A C R E A
R O L O E F G L U N G L E A A
E O E O W N A T S I N A S N J
D D U N U A C S L L E U C R S
W C T N C R C E O L N C N E E
O O O A I N T L T A U S C T L
P L A G A D E D R E I U R T K
A O S E I T N N F S E G P U N
O U J D I C G A S S N A I B I
C R T E I T W C E E G R E A R
O I C E L S O I O N C I G O P
C N F R O Y A L I C I N G E S
C G E C C N G L N E E T S E J
B A K I N G P O W D E R E W O
```

VANILLA ESSENCE   COCOA POWDER   BUTTER
CANDLES   FLOUR   FOOD COLOURING
ROYAL ICING   EGGS   SUGAR
SPRINKLES   BAKING POWDER

73

	A		F		O		Q	
	D	E	L	I	R	I	U	M
	U		O	L	D		I	
F	L	I	C	K	E	R	E	D
	T		K		R	O	T	E
A	S	P		A		S	E	E
		L		W		E	N	D
C	R	U	S	H		W		
	A	C	T	I	V	A	T	E
	S	K	E	L	E	T	A	L
	P		R	E	T	E	L	L
C	Y	A	N		O	R	C	A

The letters spell POISON.

74

```
L U R K   A P O S T A T E
I   O   O   O H   S   A
B I C Y C L E   O U S T S
E   K   C   T   R   A   T
R E S T A U R A T E U R
A     S   Y   C   L   P
T R A G I C   W I N T E R
E   C   O   L   R   E
  C O U N T E R C L A I M
E   L   A   G   U   X   O
R O Y A L   I N I T I A L
N   T   L   O   T   N   A
E V E R Y O N E   A G A R
```

ANSWERS

75

```
    D   B         T           C
T E N O R   E R O S I O N
    S   U       P   U   A   M
S T E N C I L S   S   C A M P
    I   C       O   T   C   A
U N S E E N     E T H A N E
    E       E       D   A   D
A D O P T E R   A R R O W
    L   R   R       D   I   E
L A C E S   S A I N T E D
    N   C   D       M       X
S C R I B E     S P R I T E
    E   S   A       O   E   R
I S L E     L I N E S M A N
    T   L   I       S   C   C
B R A Y I N G   G U S T O
    Y       G       E   S
```

76

Lock code: 762

8	9	⑦	2	1	5	4	6	3
3	5	1	6	8	4	7	2	9
4	6	2	3	7	9	8	5	1
2	3	8	1	⑥	7	5	9	4
9	1	4	8	5	3	6	7	2
5	7	6	9	4	②	1	3	8
6	8	3	5	2	1	9	4	7
7	2	5	4	9	8	3	1	6
1	4	9	7	3	6	2	8	5

77

49	50	52	53	74	75	85	86	97	98
48	51	54	73	76	84	87	96	100	99
47	55	71	72	77	83	88	95	94	93
46	56	67	70	78	81	82	89	92	91
45	57	66	68	69	79	80	1	90	4
44	58	60	65	64	63	38	2	3	5
29	43	59	61	62	39	37	9	8	6
28	30	42	41	40	36	35	18	10	7
26	27	31	32	33	34	19	17	14	11
25	24	23	22	21	20	16	15	13	12

78

6	1	9	8	4	7	5	3	2
2	3	5	1	6	9	8	7	4
8	4	7	3	5	2	9	1	6
4	2	3	9	8	5	7	6	1
1	9	8	6	7	3	4	2	5
7	5	6	2	1	4	3	8	9
3	6	4	5	2	8	1	9	7
5	8	1	7	9	6	2	4	3
9	7	2	4	3	1	6	5	8

79

A crossword grid with the following filled entries: ACCEPT, P, CUB; H, R, OCHRE, O; SITTING, E, D, R; A, N, R, WAITS, S; SNATCHED, L, C; T, E, S, D, L, H; LIVELY, MOZART; E, A, Y, S, G, A; T, R, APPENDIX; TRICK, A, A, S; I, O, N, WORSHIP; N, UNION, E, N; GAS, T, ODDEST

80

L	A	L	L	I	D	M	A	D	R
L	I	C	E	G	M	O	V	E	A
S	P	L	R	A	C	H	I	S	C
J	C	I	A	D	H	A	M	O	R
A	O	R	R	I	S	R	E	S	E
S	H	S	E	E	L	Y	F	Y	M
M	S	S	A	M	L	N	E	H	T
I	E	G	R	O	E	N	M	A	R
N	R	A	G	N	T	M	M	A	O
E	O	N	O	N	U	E	G	R	J

"Belladonna" is the missing word.

81

The poison was
in the drink.

82

	H		R		S		A		L		H	
G	A	Z	E	B	O		D	R	A	G	O	N
	L		I		R		M		C		P	
J	O	I	N		C	H	I	C	K	P	E	A
	F		E		X		A		L			
M	A	S	O	N	R	Y		E	D	G	E	D
	Q		R		Y		T		A		S	
Q	U	A	C	K		W	A	V	I	E	S	T
	A		E		E		B		S			
P	R	I	M	E	V	A	L		I	D	E	A
	I		E		I		E		C		M	
T	U	N	N	E	L		A	R	A	B	I	C
	M		T		S		U		L		T	

83

V	I	S	O	R	S		G		S		D	
I		P				C	R	E	A	T	I	O	N
E	R	A				R		N		R		L	
N		R	E	L	A	T	E		U	G	L	Y	
N		K		P		S		G		A			
A	R	S	O	N		D	I	G	G	E	R	S	
		V		Z		S		L					
S	I	D	E	C	A	R		J	E	R	K	S	
	N		R		M		A		A		M	
I	C	E	S		B	O	B	B	E	D		O	
	H		T		E		B		I	R	K	
B	E	D	A	Z	Z	L	E		S		E	
	S		Y		I		Y	A	C	H	T	S	

84

85

	19	18	4				12	30	
18	9	8	1	14			12	30	
27	7	9	3	8	23/3	1	2		
4	3	1	30	6	7	9	8	6	
	13	21		10/21	3	2	4	1	
3	1	2	12	8	4	9	7	2	
17	9	8	16/11	7	9	12	9	3	
10	3	1	2	4	6		9	8	
	11	3	1	2	5	3/3	2	1	
	15	7	8		11	1	2	3	5
						7	1	4	2

86

```
C O M M I S S I O N       E
O     E   E   N     P     X
C E L L U L I T E   R U T
K     O   F   I     E     E
P E N D U L U M     D O N
I     I   E   A N T I     S
T R U C K S   T     C H I
    (N)     S L E W   T   O
P O D S         M I E N
R   E   N O V A     V
O U R       U   D E S E R T
P   S I F T   M   C     I
A U K     S L O S H I N G
G   I       M   N   E   R
A I R   C A L I B R A T E
T   T       R   S   Z   S
E       M A T C H B O X E S
```

ANSWERS

87

Runner-Up in Shortbread

88

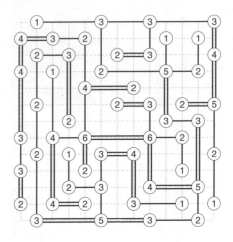

89

E	X	I	L	E		J	I	T	T	E	R	Y
X		K		X		O		R		E		
C		E		T		K		F	I	L	M	S
E	M	B	A	R	K	E	D		P		I	
L		A		E		R		A	O	R	T	A
L	A	N	D	M	A	S	S		D			F
E		A		E			Q		L			T
N		T		E	F	F	U	S	I	V	E	
T	E	P	I	D		A		I		A		R
	L		S		G	U	Z	Z	L	I	N	G
A	B	A	S	H		L		Z		S		L
	O		U			T		E		O		O
S	W	E	E	T	L	Y		S	I	N	E	W

90

9	4	7	6	5	3	2	1	8
1	5	2	7	(8)	4	3	9	6
8	6	3	9	1	2	5	7	4
5	2	1	4	6	7	9	8	3
7	3	8	2	9	1	4	6	5
6	9	4	8	3	5	1	2	7
2	8	5	3	7	9	6	4	1
3	7	9	1	4	6	8	5	2
4	1	6	5	2	8	7	3	9

91

6	9	1	7	3	5	2	4	8
4	5	9	3	8	7	1	6	2
8	4	(2)	6	9	1	7	3	5
2	8	5	1	7	3	6	9	4
3	1	6	9	5	4	8	2	7
9	2	7	4	6	8	5	1	3
5	6	4	8	2	9	3	7	1
7	3	8	2	1	6	4	5	9
1	7	3	5	4	2	9	8	6

92

1. Camilla Hague
2. Dahliah Dalliance
3. Greg Graham
4. Lucille Luck
5. Jean Hickford

93

3	5	6	4	9	8	2	7	1
4	2	7	3	5	1	8	6	9
8	1	9	2	6	7	5	3	4
7	4	8	1	3	9	6	5	2
6	9	2	7	8	5	4	1	3
5	3	1	6	4	2	9	8	7
9	7	4	8	1	6	3	2	5
2	8	3	5	7	4	1	9	6
1	6	5	9	2	3	7	4	8

94

54	55	60	61	63	65	67	68	74	75
53	56	59	62	64	66	69	73	76	77
52	57	58	23	21	20	70	72	79	78
50	51	24	22	19	15	14	71	80	81
48	49	25	18	16	3	1	13	83	82
46	47	26	17	7	4	2	12	84	85
45	44	30	27	8	6	5	11	87	86
43	42	31	29	28	9	10	94	93	88
40	41	37	32	33	100	99	95	92	89
39	38	36	35	34	98	97	96	91	90

95

Answer: The suspect lives at number 264.

96

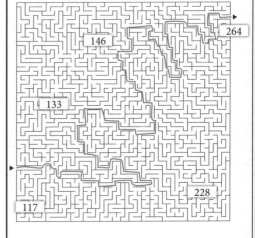

97

```
H E C T A R E S   A G U E
E   A   M   N       R   X
N O V A E   T O N S U R E
S   I   N   A       B   G
  T   D   I G N O B L E
A B Y S M A L   I   Y   T
M     E       C     I
I   M N   F R A N T I C
C O U N T E R   R   I
A   S       U   A G   S
B A S H I N G   G R E E T
L   E       A   U   R   I
Y U L E   C L E(A)N S E R
```

98

```
            12  24          11 12
         11 | 3  8 | 23      5 | 2  3
      30 20 
       8 | 8  9  7  6 |    17   8  9
    4     24        16
   24 | 1  3  24 9  8  6  1
        24        17
    | 7  9  8  18| 9  8 | 14 11
           17
        6 | 9  8 | 6 | 2  1  3
   21       7
    4 | 1  7  9  4 | 17  9  8
    5         10      14
    12| 3  2  12| (1) 2  3  4
    6         3
    | 1  3  2  18| 1  2 | 24 16
            17        15
       13| 9  8 | 24| 9  8  7
    10             16
   11| 2  1  3  4 | 3 | 7  9
    5        26
    | 2  3  | 7  8  2  9
   17              4
    | 9  8 |    | 3  1
```

CRIME 3 CONCLUSIONS

Paula Elstree was allergic to peanuts. – True

The killer had used peanuts in their cake. – Unknown

The killer came third in the previous year's baking contest. – Not true

The killer lived on the same street as Miss Hemmingway. – Not true

The message hidden in *The Puzzleby Gazette* is "Poison in the tea".

The killer is Jean Hickford.

99

The answer to the riddle is:

PHANTOM

100

9	2	4	8	1	6	5	7	3
3	6	7	5	4	9	8	2	1
8	1	3	9	2	7	4	5	6
5	9	2	6	7	8	3	1	4
7	3	1	4	9	5	2	6	8
2	4	6	1	8	3	7	9	5
1	8	5	2	6	4	9	3	7
4	7	9	3	5	1	6	8	2
6	5	8	7	3	2	1	4	9

101

```
O T B A L E R O T O V A T O R
Y W H E E L P L O U G H P R I
F R O N T E N D L O A D E R L
E E G I R C U L T I V A T O R
T I E H R O C D R S P L K W O
K F K C U R T T F I L K R O F
C I A A V K I A N L J O O R Z
O R A M K Z O G R P E W F R P
T A Y G E P H H A Y J X Y A O
T C A N T O U W W T H F A H I
A S H I O O T T B Z O O H C P
M U C K S P R E A D E R E S A
W R E L K N I R P S D L E I F
V L L I R D D E E S U O A D P
E T R M B R E T S E V R A H T
```

"Pitchfork" is the missing word.

102

TVY GVCCYR

Answer: Gil Tipple

103

B	U	M	P		P	R	O	T	E	C	T	S
A		A		P		O		H		H		U
C	O	R	P	O	R	A		I	D	I	O	M
K		G		S		S		C		G		O
B	R	E	A	T	H	T	A	K	I	N	G	
I			G		S		S		O		H	
T	H	E	I	R	S		S	K	I	N	N	Y
E		X		A		A		I		P		
	R	H	O	D	O	D	E	N	D	R	O	N
C		O		U		J		N		E		O
A	O	R	T	A		U	S	E	L	E	S	S
L		T		T		R		D		V		I
F	A	S	T	E	N	E	R		S	E	A	S

104

7	2	9	4	3	5	1	6	8
6	3	1	8	2	7	9	4	5
4	5	8	6	1	9	7	3	2
5	9	7	2	4	3	8	1	6
3	1	4	5	6	8	2	7	9
2	8	6	9	7	1	4	5	3
9	4	3	1	8	6	5	2	7
8	7	2	3	5	4	6	9	1
1	6	5	7	9	2	3	8	4

105

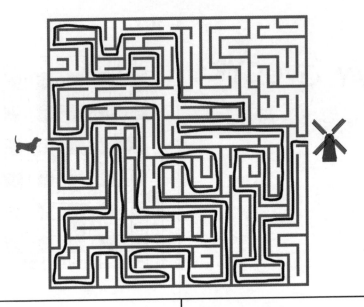

106

BETRARSWYR =
STRAWBERRY

MONFET OG ERT =
FORGET ME NOT

107

9	8	2	3	1	7	4	6	5
7	1	5	6	4	9	8	2	3
4	3	6	8	2	5	7	9	1
6	9	7	4	5	8	1	3	2
3	2	1	9	7	6	5	4	8
5	4	8	2	3	1	6	7	9
8	5	9	7	6	2	3	1	4
1	7	4	5	9	3	2	8	6
2	6	3	1	8	4	9	5	7

ANSWERS

108

P	R	E	F	I	X	E	S		E	W	E	R
O		L		D		N				A		E
S	P	A	C	E		I	N	F	U	S	E	S
E		P		A		G				H		I
		S		L		M	A	R	V	E	L	S
A	M	E	R	I	C	A		E		S		T
I				S				L				E
R		S		E		A	N	I	S	E	E	D
B	E	M	U	S	E	D		Q		S		
R		I				A		U		C		J
U	N	T	Y	I	N	G		A	Z	U	R	E
S		E				I		R		D		R
H	U	S	K		B	O	D	Y	W	O	R	K

109

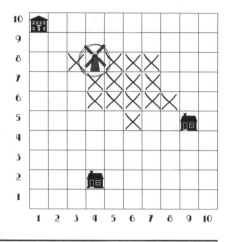

110

	H		A		B		P
	E	C	S	T	A	T	I	C
	I		P	I	T		L
O	F	F	I	C	I	A	L	S
	E		C		K	N	O	T
A	R	E		S		T	W	O
		A		O		A	S	P
A	C	T	E	D		R	
	H	E	A	D	A	C	H	E
	I	N	V	E	N	T	E	D
	M		E	N	T	I	R	E
W	E	D	S		I	C	O	N

The word scramble spells
"COFFEE SHOP"

111

U	N	A	C	C	E	P	T	A	B	L	E
N		R		U		U		N		C	
H	O	P	E	S		M		G		L	
E		E		T	R	A	D	E	S	M	A	N
S		G		A		R				I	
I		G	A	R	B		P		S	A	R	I
T		I		D	I	V	E	S	T		N	
A	N	O	N		G		B		A	U	R	A
T			O	M	N	I	B	U	S		D	
I	N	N	S		E		L		H	I	R	E
N		E	A	S	T	E	R		R		Q	
G	O	D	S		S		S	E	E	R		U
	U		A				T		I		A	
S	T	A	N	D	A	R	D	S		T		T
W			I		U		I	N	A	N	E	
I			E		M		N		N		L	
T	R	I	U	M	P	H	A	N	T	L	Y

112

T	O	T	T	E	R	E	D		O	P	U	S
O		E		X		F		E		A		P
P	L	A	N	T		F		V	E	R	S	E
S		K		R		E		O		T		E
				C	A	L	C	U	L	A	T	E	D
P		C		V		T		U		I		I
L	A	R	V	A	L		S	T	A	M	E	N
A		I		G		F		I		E		G
C	O	M	P	A	R	I	S	O	N			
A		P		N		A		N		T		S
B	L	I	T	Z		S		A	T	O	L	L
L		N		A		C		R		O		I
E	G	G	S		P	O	L	Y	G	L	O	T

113

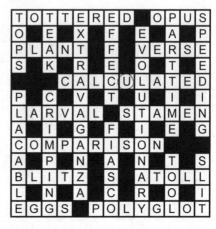

ADULT
(345 hours
after death)

♂

♀

EGGS
(0 hours
after death)

FIRST
LARVAE
STAGE
(23 hours
after death)

PUPA
(202 hours
after death)

SECOND
LARVAE STAGE
(50 hours after
death)

THIRD
LARVAE
STAGE
(72 after death)

ANSWERS

114

FRIDAY

115

M	I	M	I	C	S		S		O		S
E		A			I	N	C	U	B	A	T	E
A	W	N			E		A		L		R
G			T	R	A	V	E	L		I	C	E	D
R		R			E		L	G		E
E	X	A	C	T		S	O	C	I	E	T	Y
		O		T		P		N
R	A	I	N	B	O	W		E	G	R	E	T
	C		J		P		Q			E		W
Z	E	B	U		S	M	U	D	G	E		I
	T		N		P		I		K	E	N
M	I	S	C	H	I	E	F			E		G
	C		T		N		F	O	N	D	L	E

116

O	P	E	R	A	T	E	D		E	P	E	E
N		G		S		C			R		N
Y	A	R	N	S		H	A	Z	I	E	S	T
X		E		U		O			F		R
		S		R		E	S	Q	U	I	R	E
J	E	S	T	E	R	S		U		X		A
A			D			I			T
V		A		L		S	U	B	S	I	D	Y
E	N	C	R	Y	P	T		B		M
L		U			R		L		P		B
I	M	M	E	R	S	E		I	M	A	G	E
N		E			W		N		C		V
S	A	N	K		K	N	I	G	H	T	L	Y

265

ANSWERS

117

8	7	6	5	4	3	2	59	60	61
9	10	14	15	16	1	58	64	63	62
11	13	18	17	36	37	57	65	67	68
12	19	33	35	38	44	56	66	70	69
20	32	34	39	43	45	55	74	73	71
21	31	40	42	46	54	80	79	75	72
22	30	41	47	53	81	91	92	78	76
23	29	48	52	82	90	93	94	95	77
24	28	49	51	83	86	89	96	98	100
25	26	27	50	84	85	87	88	97	99

118

```
B U F F S   P I N H O L E
A   I   A   O       M   N
C R E A S E D   V   I   G
K   L   H   S   E   T   I
B   D   A     S L O T   N
I   W   Y E W   T   E K E
T O O       A   E Y E D   E
E   R E A R           R
    K     N A P     A
M         A P E S     S
E   K E R B   N     P E P
C H I   A   A T E   A   O
H   N A V Y     Y   R   R
A   S   I   W   R   T   T
N   H   O   O R I G A M I
I   I   L   K   E   M   V
C A P S I Z E   S I E V E
```

The word scramble spells
"GIL TIPPLE"

119

| 15 | 9 | 8 | | | 19 | 30 |
Across/Down answers (filled cells):

- 7: 4 2 1
- 30: 8 6 7 9
- 17 / 21 clues: 8 9
- 4: 3 1
- 29: 7 8 9 (5)
- 11 / 10: 3 2 1 5
- 16: 7 9   4: 3 1   16: 7 9
- 4: 1 3   10 / 18: 1 9   15: 8 7
- 28: 8 7 9 4
- 26: 8 7 2 9   4 / 4: 3 1
- 3: 1 2   27: 8 3 7 9
- 6: 1 2 3

ANSWERS

120

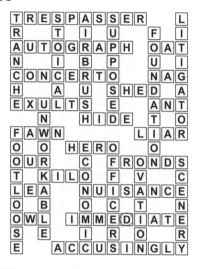

121

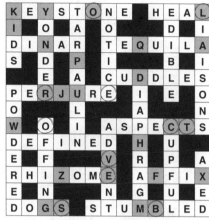

The word scramble spells
"LOBSTER COVE"

122

DEP: THURSDAY 6.28 PM
RETURN: FRIDAY 1.39 PM

742123

6	5	4	2	7	3	9	8	1
8	2	1	9	6	4	5	7	3
9	7	3	5	8	1	6	2	4
3	4	5	6	2	8	1	9	7
7	8	6	1	3	9	2	4	5
2	1	9	4	5	7	8	3	6
4	6	8	7	9	5	3	1	2
5	3	7	8	1	2	4	6	9
1	9	2	3	4	6	7	5	8

ANSWERS

123

```
      S           L
U S E     S     U S A
    H E A T     K E N
    O P P O N E N T
    W E E N     W O E
A N D       Y E A R N
                R A N
    S C R E A M       A
    L O A Ⓜ           I
D E T R I M E N T
    E   E R R A T A
    T O R   S T O P
```

124

9	2	4	8	6	1	5	7	3
6	1	5	7	2	3	9	8	4
7	8	3	4	9	5	2	6	1
2	4	7	1	8	9	3	5	6
1	5	8	3	7	6	4	9	2
3	9	6	5	4	2	8	1	7
4	6	1	2	5	8	7	3	9
8	7	9	6	3	4	1	2	5
5	3	2	⑨	1	7	6	4	8

125

MENU

CUCUMBER SANDWICHES

APRICOT TARTS

BLUEBERRY MUFFINS

RASPBERRY SHORTCAKE

BLACKBERRY JAM

126

Nellie Yore

127

O	C	H	E		C	O	N	T	R	A	C	T
C		O		P		L		O		R		O
C	O	V	E	R	E	D		G	A	M	M	Y
U		E		O			E		H			S
P	O	L	E	P	O	S	I	T	I	O	N	
I				O		P		H		L		R
E	L	L		R	E	U	S	E		E	G	O
D		O		T		R		R				L
	I	N	D	I	S	T	I	N	C	T	L	Y
O		G		O			E		U		P	
S	T	E	R	N		R	I	S	O	T	T	O
L		S		A		A		S		O		L
O	N	T	O	L	O	G	Y		A	R	M	Y

128

ANSWERS

129

130

5	4	3	2	1	21	22	36	37	38
6	7	11	12	20	23	35	44	40	39
8	10	13	19	24	34	46	45	43	41
9	14	18	25	33	47	48	49	50	42
15	17	26	32	57	56	55	54	53	51
16	27	31	58	91	98	99	80	79	52
28	30	59	90	92	100	97	96	81	78
29	60	68	89	93	94	95	85	82	77
61	64	67	69	88	87	86	84	83	76
62	63	65	66	70	71	72	73	74	75

131

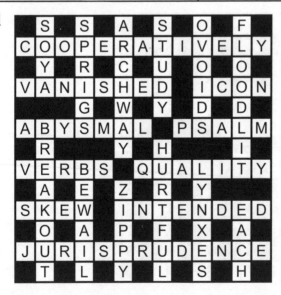

132

7.15am Meet Sam Haggle at mill (remember keys)

133

```
P L U S R E P P O C
H B U B U E R D E R
A N N N R N S L O H
T O S E C E T I M P
E I T L Y L B R A L
G O U I N C I R E C
G L E D U R I C N
L S O R T D C N L A
E L E N E O R G A B
S F U N S T T U B E
```

134

```
E  E     A     B        W     A
M A L A Y S I A    B R A N       O
B  E     S     G        E     O
A  V     A     E  P I N T     T  D
T  A     S K I    C O Y          Y
T U T O R S    P O S H        N  E
L  O     E     E        E        E
E A R T H S    R U E D
D     U           L           E
   E B B S    T I L I N G        O
N  S     U     H        N     O
I  C L U B    A N O I N T        T
B O A       T O N        T     I
B  P I E R    K           I     S
L  I     A     I           A    T
E L S E    C O N F E T T I
D     T     T     G        E     C
```

ANSWERS

135

	A		T		C		
T	R	U	T	H		O	N	E
	T		O		N	A	Y
P	I	R	O	U	E	T	T	E
	S	E	W	S		R	I	D
	T	E	L	A	V	I	V	
H	E	X		N		B	E	E
	A	D	D		U		G
D	E	M	I		S	T	I	R
	I	N	V	O	I	C	E
T	U	N	A		F	O	E	S
	E	R	R	A	N	D	S

136

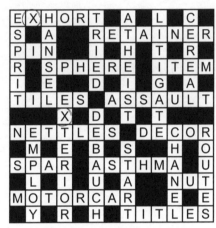

The gender profile is XX.

CRIME 4 CONCLUSIONS

The murderer was a man. – Not true

Gil Tipple was not in Puzzleby at the time of the murder. – True

The murderer drove the victim to the haunted mill. – Unknown

Before the murder, the Puzzleby Historical Society was going out of business. – True

The message hidden in *The Puzzleby Gazette* is "The haunted mill keys".

The killer is Nellie Yore.

137

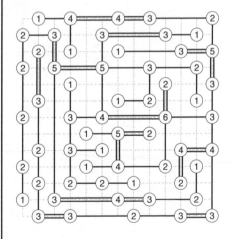

ANSWERS

138

HINT: this is not A1 Z26!

$$123$$
$$+302$$
$$=425$$

Key 425 opens the lock.

139

S		S		J				C		C		P
I	S	O	B	A	R		C	O	R	O	N	A
X		M		Z		P		N		R		V
F	R	E	E	Z	E	R		S	I	N	C	E
O		H		Y		E		O		Y		D
L	O	O	K			I	D	O	L	S		
D		W		R		A		E		C		H
		M	E	E	T	S		P	U	P	A	
O		F		Q		O		W		B		G
B	I	J	O	U		R	A	I	N	I	N	G
O		O		I		Y		N		C		L
E	R	R	A	T	A		O	C	T	A	V	E
S		D		E				H		L		D

140

2	3	4	10	11	21	22	23	24	25
1	5	9	12	20	31	30	29	28	26
6	8	13	19	32	68	67	63	62	27
7	14	18	33	81	80	69	66	64	61
15	17	34	93	92	82	79	70	65	60
16	35	94	100	98	91	83	78	71	59
36	46	95	97	99	90	84	77	72	58
37	45	47	96	89	88	85	76	73	57
38	41	44	48	87	86	75	74	56	55
39	40	42	43	49	50	51	52	53	54

ANSWERS

141

142

8	1	4	5	7	6	3	2	9
7	6	9	1	2	3	5	4	8
3	5	2	8	9	4	1	6	7
1	4	8	2	3	9	6	7	5
2	9	7	4	6	5	8	1	3
6	3	5	7	8	1	2	9	4
4	2	1	9	5	8	7	3	6
9	8	3	6	1	7	4	5	2
5	7	6	3	4	2	9	8	1

143

ANSWERS

144

SERMONS

PSALMS

FETE

(FINANCES)

VICARAGE

PHOTOS

145

- Withdraw 1/3 of the original pretty cash for church repairs to fund the roof - $750
- Use 2/3 of this amount for the labor and tiles - $500. Keep 1/3 for contingency.
- Total church funds - $2,250
- Loss - 1/3 roof funds - $250

146

3	4	2	9	8	1	5	7	6
6	5	7	3	2	4	1	9	8
9	8	1	6	5	7	2	4	3
4	6	9	5	1	2	8	3	7
7	1	8	4	6	3	9	5	2
5	2	3	7	9	8	6	1	4
1	7	5	2	3	6	4	8	9
8	3	6	1	4	9	7	2	5
2	9	4	8	7	5	3	6	1

147

```
W R E N C H       T E M P O
I     X   O           O   R
N A T A N T   V E R S E D
  E   D   E   P   X   I   N
  D   O   N   E   A   I   I N C
O N S     P R I S M   V I A N
W S   S K I R T   N       E   N C
S K I R T   O   T   P   L     N C E
K O       T I N T S   E L O P E
T I N T S   A     H   A       I
A   C   S   H U   K   S I N C E
C   T I P   F A I N T     T   S
T   A   F   N   I     M E   S C U
I   T   L   G   M     E     C U
C   I N U R E S   T U R N E D   T O
A       L           L         T O
N E A R S       K I S S E S
```

148

Deacon Beacon

149

```
    A           T       D
    P A C K A G E S
H E R O       U R N
      E M U       E       Y
    M A P       M E M O
      A       E C R U
V I B R A T E S
    L O T               A
    L A M B S K I N
    S T E A L I N G
      E N G U L F S
H U R T       M O O T
```

150

2	7	6	8	4	9	5	3	1
8	3	9	5	6	1	7	2	4
4	5	1	2	3	7	9	8	6
1	4	2	3	9	8	6	7	5
5	8	3	7	1	6	4	9	2
6	9	7	4	5	2	8	1	3
3	1	5	9	8	4	2	6	7
9	2	4	6	7	3	1	5	8
7	6	8	1	2	5	3	4	9

151

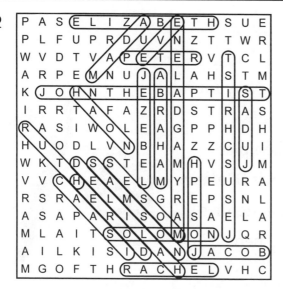

152

ANSWERS

153

```
  P   D   Q   W   C   B
M I L I E U   E X H A(L)E
  N   F   A   I   E   O
S E L F   F E R V E N C Y
    E   F   S   R   K
T E R R I E R   G L E A M
  L   E   D   A   E   D
P O I N T   S M A S H E D
  Q   T   Z   P   S
J U D I C I A L   N E C K
  E   A   P   I   E   L
I N S T E P   F U S I O N
  T   E   Y   Y   S   T
```

154

2	5	1	6	7	4	3	8	9
9	4	3	1	8	2	5	6	7
6	8	7	3	2	5	4	9	1
7	1	4	9	6	3	8	2	5
8	3	5	4	(9)	7	2	1	6
5	6	2	8	1	9	7	4	3
1	7	9	2	5	8	6	3	4
3	2	6	7	4	1	9	5	8
4	9	8	5	3	6	1	7	2

155

Miss Hemmingway found:

- A broken plate
- Some shards of glass
- Some fishing flies
- Some pens

156

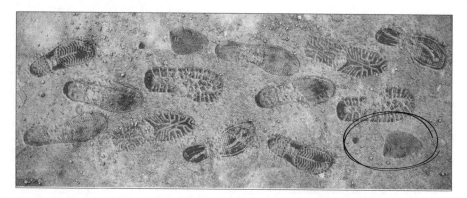

The footprints match up, except for one mystery high-heel footprint.

157

158

E	L	L	I	P	T	I	C	A	L			S		
N			S		R		R				R	U		
A	L	L	O	C	A	T	E	D		E	G	G		
B			M		V		D				F	G		
L	I	T	E	R	A	T	I				L	Y	E	
E			R		I			T	I	R	E	S		
D	A	M	S	E	L		O				C	O	T	
		O			S	A	R	I			T	E		
S	U	N	K						W	I	N	D		
C		U		I	C	E	D			V				
H	E	M		L		I	M	P	E	L	S			
O		E	A	S	E		S		R		U			
O	W	N			A	P	P	E	A	S	E	R		
L		T			N		R		I			G		
B	O	A		L	I	M	O	U	S	I	N	E		
O		L			N		V		E			O		
Y			D	I	G	R	E	S	S	I	O	N		

ANSWERS

159

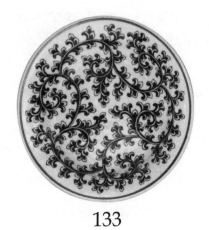

133

160

STOP
iNVES tiGaTiNG
tHe muRdeR
oF father
   feaTHErby
or tHE CaT
GeTs it

161

6	7	5	1	3	8	9	4	2
4	1	2	6	5	9	3	8	7
3	9	8	4	2	7	1	6	5
7	4	6	3	8	1	2	5	9
2	3	1	5	9	4	6	7	8
5	8	9	2	7	6	4	1	3
9	2	4	7	1	5	8	3	6
1	5	3	8	6	2	7	9	4
8	6	7	9	4	3	5	2	1

ANSWERS

162

	A		S			G	
	S	C	H	O	L	A	R	S
S	H	O	E			T	O	P
		P	L	A	C	E	B	O
		E	L	F		W	O	K
D	I	S	S	I	P	A	T	E
			E		Y		N
P	E	A	R	L	S		U
	P	R	E	D	I	C	T	S
	E	M	U		L	A	T	E
B	E	E	S		O	P	E	N
		D	E	S	S	E	R	T

163

164

4	3	2	1	15	16	17	18	19	20
5	7	8	14	87	86	46	45	22	21
6	9	13	95	96	88	85	47	44	23
10	12	94	97	98	89	84	48	43	24
11	78	93	100	99	90	83	49	42	25
74	77	79	92	91	82	59	50	41	26
73	75	76	80	81	60	58	51	40	27
67	72	71	70	61	57	52	39	34	28
66	68	69	62	56	53	38	35	33	29
65	64	63	55	54	37	36	32	31	30

165

4	7	2	6	1	5	8	9	3
8	1	9	3	5	7	2	4	6
3	6	5	2	8	4	9	1	7
7	9	6	4	3	2	5	8	1
5	2	8	1	6	9	7	3	4
2	3	7	8	9	1	4	6	5
9	4	1	5	7	6	3	2	8
6	5	3	9	4	8	1	7	2
1	8	4	7	2	3	6	5	9

166

167

HINT:
1/M, 7/D, Right +2, means "start on square M:1, then go along 2 squares to the right".

Following this method, you get:

GSFEFSJDL CBJMFZ = FREDERICK BAILEY

NBDL DIBUUFSMFZ = MACK CHATTERLEY

KFBO IJDLGPSE = JEAN HICKFORD

OFMMJF ZPSF = NELLIE YORE

ANSWERS

168

4	5	8	9	6	7	2	1	3
7	3	2	5	8	1	6	4	9
6	1	9	2	3	4	8	7	5
9	2	4	6	7	5	3	8	1
5	7	6	3	1	8	9	2	4
3	8	1	4	9	2	5	6	7
1	9	7	8	5	6	4	3	2
2	6	5	7	4	3	1	9	8
8	4	3	1	2	9	7	5	6

169

170

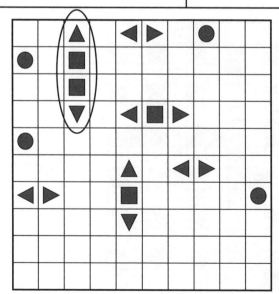

ANSWERS

171

1

172

```
COINCIDENTAL
I   G   O O O     O
VENOM   L   I     C
I   O   BEEFSTEAK
L   R   I     Y   T
I ACNE   V DIET
S N GYRATE   R
ANTE   E C ARIA
T     VILLAIN   N
IDLE   I T SETS
O   NODDED X   M
NETS   S   DRAT I
R   S     A   E S
HAMSTRING   R S
S   E C ORIBI
E   E E O O O
RHODODENDRON
```

173

```
PARALLEL   WAKE
 B  N   I   O   H   N
HAGGIS   YEOMEN
 L  L   TEA   E   E
ZONE   E   LIVELY
 N     N     E
DETERS   JARRED
   M     E     N
STRUNG   QUAY
 O  L  AFT  U  B
OXTAIL   EDIBLE
 I  T   E  R  T  E
ACRE   SUSPENSE
```

ANSWERS

174

175

	P			I		A		
	P	R	E	S	T	R	A	I	N
N	O	A	H		E	L	M	
		R	A	G		K		A
	I	L	K		B	A	B	Y
		E		A	L	O	E	
A	I	R	S	T	R	I	P	
	N	A	P					T
	C	R	E	O	S	O	T	E
	H	E	A	D	A	C	H	E
		F	R	E	S	H	E	N
S	K	Y	E		H	E	N	S

176

2	9	8	6	7	4	1	5	3
4	1	3	5	9	8	6	2	7
7	5	6	3	2	1	9	8	4
3	4	5	1	6	2	7	9	8
6	7	2	8	5	9	3	4	1
1	8	9	7	4	3	2	6	5
9	3	7	2	8	5	4	1	6
8	2	1	4	3	6	5	7	9
5	6	4	9	1	7	8	3	2

ANSWERS

177

The Deacon is
being troublesome.
He won't have his
fortune told. But I can
pin it on him anyway.
Signed:
Achillia Headland

178

Bananas

Doorstop

Belladonna

Pitchfork

179

M		C			Z		U			L		G
A	D	O	P	T	I	O	N		Z	E	T	A
T		N			M		C			G		R
R		V			B		O	R	C	A		A
I		U			A	R	M			L	U	G
A	P	L	O	M	B		M	A	G	I		E
R		S			W		O			T		S
C	R	E	A	S	E		N	O	S	Y		
H			S						A			A
		C	H	I	C		H	A	G	G	I	S
B		H			L		I			R		P
O		A	U	R	A		D	E	L	E	T	E
W	A	S			S	H	E			E		R
L		T	I	E	S		A			T		S
I		E			I		W			I		I
N	I	N	E		F	L	A	M	I	N	G	O
E		S			Y		Y			G		N

ANSWERS

180

U	G	A	N	D	A		A		M		P	
R		N		B	A	D	G	E	R	E	D	
B	U	T		I		D		R		S		
A		H	A	N	D	E	L		I	D	E	A
N		E		E		I		N		T		
E	G	R	E	T		A	N	A	G	R	A	M
		V		B		G		U				
D	U	T	I	F	U	L		D	E	C	O	Y
	S		D		R		S		R			E
D	U	P	E		S	E	T	T	L	E		A
	R		N		A		E		A	I	R	
S	P	E	C	T	R	U	M		T		N	
	S		E		S		S	E	V	E	N	S

181

5	6	7	1	3	4	2	9	8
8	2	1	6	7	9	5	4	3
4	9	3	8	2	5	6	7	1
2	7	4	3	9	6	8	1	5
6	3	8	5	4	1	7	2	9
1	5	9	7	8	2	3	6	4
7	1	6	4	5	3	9	8	2
9	8	5	2	1	7	4	3	6
3	4	2	9	6	8	1	5	7

CRIME 5 CONCLUSIONS

The mastermind met with each of the murderers before the victims' deaths. – True

The Deacon was embezzling funds meant for the church roof. – Not true

The Deacon refused to have his fortune told. – True

The message hidden in *The Puzzleby Gazette* is "Look, MH! Achillia Headland is an anagram!"

ANSWERS

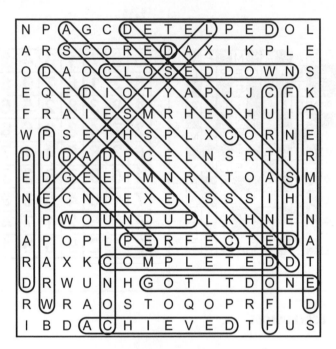

N P A G C D E T E L P E D O L
A R S C O R E D A X I K P L E
O D A O C L O S E D D O W N S
E Q E D I O T Y A P J J C F K
F R A I E S M R H E P H U I T
W P S E T H S P L X C O R N E
D U D A D P C E L N S R T I R
E D G E E P M N R I T O A S M
N E C N D E X E I S S S I H I
I P W O U N D U P L K H N E N
A P O P L P E R F E C T E D A
R A X K C O M P L E T E D D T
D R W U N H G O T I T D O N E
R W R A O S T O Q O P R F I D
I B D A C H I E V E D T F U S